GENERATION GIVE

GENERATION GIVE

TIM AZZOLINI

NEW DEGREE PRESS

COPYRIGHT © 2018 TIM AZZOLINI

GENERATION GIVE

ISBN   978-1-64137-036-3   *Paperback*

ISBN   978-1-64137-037-0   *Ebook*

CONTENTS

INTRODUCTION

When Neil Blumenthal graduated from Tufts University in 2002, he decided to take a job that he felt would give him the ability to give back to the community. While many of his friends took lucrative jobs on Wall Street or in Silicon Valley, Neil took a job at a nonprofit organization called VisionSpring. "VisionSpring is a social enterprise that trains low-income women and men to start their own businesses selling affordable eyeglasses to impoverished individuals in developing countries" (Schawbel).

After five years, Blumenthal left VisionSpring to go to business school at Wharton. Some might call such a diametrical move opposed to the 'give first' approach he expressed during those five years in the nonprofit sector. However, for Neil it was a necessary step in his efforts to combine his passion for both business and doing good.

Inspired by a passing conversation about the necessity of seeing in the modern world, Blumenthal, along with four close friends he met in business school, founded the eyeglasses retailer, Warby Parker, in 2010. In an interview with *Business Insider* from April 2017, Blumenthal characterizes the company as an attempt to create a vertically integrated brand. After consecutive features in Vogue and GQ, the business took off exponentially. In 2015 Fast Company recognized Warby Parker as the most innovative company in the world. Today Warby Parker is the number one store for millennials, and currently valued at over one billion dollars.

What's their secret to success? The company is anything but a sell-out of Blumenthal's 'do good' approach. Through a partnership with VisionSpring, for every pair of glasses sold, Warby Parker commits to training a new low-income entre-preneur on how to start his or her own business in his or her own community. Blumenthal highlights, "One of the things that we decided early on was that, we're building a brand and a brand is not just a logo. It's not just a visual identity. A brand is a point of view and that point of view needs to be lived. It really comes down to the culture of the company" (Warby Parker).

This idea of living a point of view is a schema that is funda-mentally revolutionizing business and consumer practices on a global scale. The genius of Blumenthal is the hallmark of the millennial mind. Yet what exactly *is* the millennial mind and how did we get here? Why is this so-called 'do-good model' so effective, and how can we foster it into a movement?

What exactly does Warby Parker do differently that has made them so innovative? Lots of companies have corporate social responsibility programs. Plenty of companies donate money to charities and people in need. And we've seen hundreds of different approaches to corporations "giving back." But why have Warby Parker, Toms, Cotopaxi and others captured lightning in a bottle, changing the entire mindset of giving back?

*   *

A LETTER TO MILLENNIALS

We buy things that we want from companies we admire, harboring this notion that we are making our lives incrementally better, all while fulfilling our civic duty to contribute to the economy. Every once in a while we like to donate to the little tip jar, clink a quarter into the empty water bottle next to the register, leave an extra dollar at the lemonade stand on the corner…just to add a little extra "feel-good" to our purchase. Then we carry on with our day, not knowing—or even particularly caring—how that quarter or dollar affected the life of someone else. At the end of the day, we are sold on the idea that we are bettering our own lives.

What if I told you that this is changing?

Your parents are sitting in an Econ 101 lecture and the professor is talking about business ethics. He mentions a current legal action being taken against an oil company in the Gulf. They wonder if they will ever go to Florida. They wonder about the chemical composition of oil. Someone asks the professor to expand on the case. He doesn't have time; they have to move on. Their legal pads are covered with scribbles of blue pen. Your father is drawing a picture of your professor as a clown.

You're sitting in your Econ 101 discussion and the professor is talking about business ethics. He briefly mentions a current legal action being taken against an oil company in Texas. You google "Texas oil" and spend the rest of the class reading about Talisman Energy and their involvement in a class-action suit.

Because of the Internet, because of mass globalization and its subsequent effects on education and societal norms, our generation approaches all different sorts of markets uniquely. This is the reason why companies like Warby Parker, Charity Water, and TOMS Shoes have experienced exponential success in comparison to the previously dominating companies in their industries: the unification of mass culture. Increased accessibility to information, company practices, social activism, and political campaigns has allowed, in

essence, anyone in the world to unite and begin a movement…
seemingly overnight.

In businesses like Warby Parker, products no longer have
a singular definition but, rather, have become physical
manifestations for a myriad of connotations. The roots of
materialism have been interwoven with millennial emphasis
on individual idealism.

In 2015, the annual Nielson Global Corporate Sustainability
Report indicated that, globally, 66% of consumers are willing to spend more on a product if it comes from a sustainable
brand. Seventy-three percent of surveyed millennials indicated a similar preference. Even more so, 81% of millennials
expected their favorite companies to make public declarations
of their "corporate citizenship." This expectation stems from
individual values, and the recognition of this multivalence, not
only in consumerism, but also in the workplace, in schools,
and in home life. This shift, in turn, puts pressure on businesses and companies to adhere to a deeper set of standards
than before, that *a more global society* prescribes. Essentially,
media and communication have given the consumer a new
kind of autonomy. In this coming age of the conscious
consumer and worker, companies that create a connection,
that believe in what we believe, and that have an impact, are
the ones that are prevailing, the ones that are at the forefront
of movements, the ones attracting the best and the brightest.

This idealism also affects the millennial worker. A survey done recently at YPulse found that 76% of millennials would "rather have a career they are passionate about but doesn't earn a lot of money than have a high earning career that they are not passionate about." Andersen says, "I've seen this too: for most millennials, if they don't feel a personal connection to their work, they'll see it as a temporary way to put food on the table and pay the rent while they look for something that's more meaningful to them" (Andersen).

Why are we so dissatisfied?

"What do you want to do?" we ask.

"I want to do what I love," we respond.

What is it that we love? We are always asking this privileged question. I want to argue that we aren't so much responding from a place of personal interest that reflects our narcissism as compared to that of earlier generations, but rather that we are responding to a modern pressure to be creative, to be unique.

This pressure is not misplaced. In fact, it's what I think will drive industry into a promising, globally-conscious, and consistently innovative future. To accept creativity is to accept evolution. Essentially, we have an obligation, don't we? Presented with this new and constantly evolving set of tools, our generation—more than any other, it seems—is the key to a progressively transparent, ethical, inclusive, and high-functioning marketplace. Not only do we have the ability, I would argue that we have the obligation to sit in an Econ class and look up the word our professor didn't explain. We have an obligation to cite the Prime Minister of England in a paper on the Ethics of the American Oil Consumption. We have an obligation to click a link on Wikipedia that leads us to a completely unrelated, yet interconnected topic. These jumps of association will help us reconcile our individuality in a consuming culture, and foster space to house those light bulb moments, just like the one that created Warby Parker.

*   *

THE CORPORATE MISSION MODEL

This book is for anyone and everyone who has used the word "millennial," or has been confused by the millennial mind. This book is also for anyone who believes they already understand the millennial.

This book will attempt to explain the new model of CSR— Corporate Social Responsibility 2.0. Having studied dozens and dozens of successful companies practicing the Corporate Mission Model, we've found a set of traits, patterns and activities they have in common. And, likewise, we've seen a number of 'copycats' who've tried to shoehorn the Corporate Mission Model into their businesses and failed miserably.

You'll learn:

- How a reality show contestant was able to harness the power of the crowd to create a revolution in footwear called TOMS Shoes.
- How the world's most serious problems, like malnutrition, poverty, and access to education are being solved by businesses, not just philanthropy.
- How the B Corp status became a tool for upstart brands, like Cotopaxi, to stand out in a crowded market.

Ultimately you'll find that millennial is not just an adjective, but wholly its own intricate concept. This book is aimed at the next generation of entrepreneurs, business executives, CEOs and innovators who don't want to choose. Like Neil Blumenthal, they are looking for a way *not* to sell out, but to sell more and give more back. And perhaps at no time in human history have we been poised for this time of revolution.

*   *

The Corporate Mission Model has the potential to transform our world, but it's not as simple as:

- Giving one away with each purchase
- Donating money and sharing it on social media
- Adding a 'donate here' button on your website and agreeing to match donations
- Or even promoting a Corporate Social Responsibility Program

This model requires much more to make it work, and it is much easier to cause it to fail. Read on to meet real individuals who've taken to heart what it means to be a millennial. Let a wildly successful, yet often overlooked, generation inspire you to let the do-good model work for you, to let concepts breath, and to find those spaces of innovation in places of purpose and unexpected associations.

CHAPTER 1

UNDERSTANDING THE MILLENNIAL MIND

———

I sat on my bed with my laptop, a notepad and my phone, anxiously waiting for Ari Krasner to call, the founder and CEO of GiveButter. I had some notes and questions written out in case I blanked.

The phone rang.

ARI: This is Ari, is this Tim?

ME: Yep, this is Tim. How's it going?

ARI: It's been good. You're at the University of Michigan, right? How do you like it there?

ME: It's been awesome. Tons of new and driven people.

Professors are cool, classes are good. Always something to do.

ARI: That's awesome. I wasn't so much a fan of school. So it's always good to hear why people like it. So let's get into it, tell me about this book of yours.

This was the opening to my conversation with an up-and-coming social Entrepreneur and singer/songwriter, Ari Krasner. Ari is a student at The George Washington University who loves business, loves music even more, and plans to use both to change the world. While we shared different opinions, we found a common passion for business models that have found innovative ways to give back.

Ari has mixed his passion for business with his passion for giving back. GiveButter, Ari's social crowdfunding platform, boasts the lowest fees in the industry, excellent team fundraising standards, and a huge representation of 300+ ambassadors across college campuses. Givebutter charges a start-up fee of 0.5%, which is much lower compared to other fundraising sites. Possibly, though, the largest difference between GiveButter and other fundraising sites is that GiveButter has taken the fundraising industry a step further by connecting the campaigns launched on their site to a community of people seeking to give. More so, GiveButter has set up a platform that clearly lays out the acute impact that each campaign is making. For example, the "Students for Orphan Relief at OU" raises money to send orphaned children in Ghana to school, and the campaign clearly lays out how the $20 (or more) that you donate will fund part of one child's tuition in Ghana (Brucella).

The motivation behind its success is in its motto: Eat. Sleep. Give.

And the story behind its creation sums up how an aspirational generation of students, entrepreneurs, and visionaries are changing the giving landscape. Ari and his co-founders found that that community was millennials, and targeted them early on. But before I get into that, we need to first understand why the millennial mind is so eager to give.

*   *

WHO ARE WE

Have you ever noticed that a lot of the media out there on millennials is not actually written or told *by* millennials? Most of the articles and news loves to quote statistics, as they openly debate how to define a generation. It's like they've discovered a new species, and can't tell if it's dangerous or not.

While I cannot speak on the behalf of all millennials, I can't help but offer my insights as someone who is defined as a millennial in the workplace. I'm sure most of us are familiar with the "millennials in the workplace" discussion that brings along a whole slew of generalizing terms like: Lazy, incompetent, always-asking-for-help, addicted-to-technology, and indecisive. Honestly, though, if we take a step back and dive a little deeper into what has made this generation so different, is pretty simple.

First, the term millennial encompasses a significantly larger age range than that which it is often associated. The U.S. Census Bureau define Millennials as those from the ages of 18-34 (in 2015), a group that is comprised of 75.4 million people, surpassing the 74.9 million Baby Boomers defined as ages 51-69. Mixed in there are Generation X, defined as ages 35-50 (in 2015). But still, not everyone agrees with this definition of millennials; some feel it is too broad, and should be narrowed into more specific characteristics. Take Jesse Singal, author of the CNN article, "The Science of Us."

She writes, " In 2015, for example, Juliet Lapidos—born the same year I was—may have put it best in a column for the *New York Times* headlined 'Wait, What, I'm a Millennial?'—'I don't identify with the kids that *Time* magazine described as technology-addled narcissists, the Justin Bieber fans who "boomerang" back home instead of growing up,' she writes. And I've had plenty of conversations with other people my age who feel the same way. Many, many people who are in their late 20s and early 30s simply don't feel like they are a part of the endlessly dissected millennial generation."

So is it right to paint millennials with such a broad brush, when it is clear that we really aren't sure exactly what age we are talking about? The millennial age-range, after all, is very broad, and so, given that fact, and for the sake of using the word "millennial" moving forward, I'd like to define, to the best of my ability, the question: Who are we? (Singal)

WE ARE UNSETTLERS AND ITERATORS

Due to a massive amount of exposure and information all around us, opportunities seem endless. We usually don't settle for a the first job we get or buy into the work your way up mentality. While there are pros to that approach it is often not the job that was dreamed about as a kid and the work in unfulfilling. Unsettling is actively learning. Learning about ourselves and about new things, new professions, and new environments that push forward our passions. When the work we do does not align with an environment that allows us to thrive, we are willing to iterate. And it's not that we are not loyal to the company that spent time hiring us and fostering young professionals, it's just that we aren't willing to give up the purpose we set out to find.

In a Deloitte study on "Millennials in the Workplace," research shows that rarely does the decision to walk away have anything to do with money. Actually, opportunity and purpose are usually the focus. Secondly, it means that if we're sticking with you, we're *really* with you.

And there are the lucky few of us that find that purpose in high school or college and rarely iterate. But for many of us, it's not that we aren't up for the challenge, its that we would rather bet on the risk of chasing another opportunity aligned closely with our values, or in an environment that allows us to thrive. And for that, we don't settle, we iterate.

*　*

ANTI-PROFIT BIAS

We can see that Capitalism can be harnessed for a greater good, not a greater gain. Ralph Waldo Emerson sums this up well, saying, "Doing well is the result of doing good. That's what Capitalism is all about."

Millennials are part of a perfect storm that consists of a population of people entering and establishing themselves in the work force, people who are highly mobile and active, extremely capable, and deeply value- and purpose- driven. These values are a secret weapon to facing chronic social challenges and creating change through business. And while millennials may be bringing strong values to the table, our generation's anti-profit bias is a huge obstacle facing our generation.

Earlier in the summer I was sent an article about this bias, in which the cover showed a young protestor welding a sign reading, "FUCK CAPITALISM"; it definitely hits home that there is a deep anger towards the capitalist society. I've experienced this anger in friends and colleagues, I experienced it throughout my high school years, and I experience often here at school in Michigan.

In a Forbes study where participants rated Fortune 500 companies in terms of how profitable they thought they were and how much they thought they engaged in bad business practices, such as operating at the expense of others with no concern for society, it was found that when, "Participants rated Fortune 500 companies in terms of how profitable they thought they were and how much they thought they engaged in bad business practices, such as operating at the expense of others with no concern for society. There was a clear pattern: the more profitable participants thought a company was, the more they assumed that it engaged in more bad business practices" (Jarrett).

And while there is this ingrained profit bias in a large percentage of millennials, there is a lack of understanding of how capitalism is changing, because we are demanding it change.

The biggest thing that we fail to recognize is basic macro-economics: that market forces operate on a "massive scale, in which for-profit companies competing in a free market with informed customers need to innovate, behave fairly and develop a good reputation in order to be profitable over the long term." It's on us to keep pushing our standards on companies, and in order to compound this effect, new companies need to start out at this standard in order to stay competitive with a millennial consumer base demanding these practices and values. And it's awesome to see that companies and entrepreneurs are answering this demand.

Amit Bhattacharjee, author and professor at Erasmus University, believes this anti-profit bias leads many voters and politicians to endorse anti-profit policies that are likely to lead to the very opposite outcomes for society that they want to achieve. "Erroneous anti-profit beliefs may lead to systematically worse economic policies for society, even as they help people satisfy their social and expressive needs on an individual level" (Jarrett).

*   *

STATS IN THE WORKPLACE

The average time that millennials stay at a company is two years. By the definition of a professional career, two years is nothing compared to the average of Baby Boomer employees which is seven years. (Fromm) To get an even better look at this changing dynamic, take a look at these stats provided by:

- There are currently 40 million millennials in the workplace
- By 2025, 3 out of every 4 workers will be Millennials
- 45% of millennials will choose workplace flexibility over pay
- 54% either want to start a business or have already started one
- 77% of millennials said it was important to for them to attend frequent face-to-face meetings
- 84% of millennials say making a difference in the world is more important than professional recognition
- 89% of millennials would prefer to choose when and where they work, rather than being placed in a 9-to-5 position
- 90% of millennials surveyed think being an entrepreneur means having a certain mindset, rather than starting a company
- 92% of millennials believe businesses should be measured by more than their profits (OfficeVibe)

So we can see that Millennials are always on the lookout for opportunities that align with their values and advance their professional careers. Millennials are a fast moving generation and have adopted an entrepreneurial mindset. And the digital age has fostered this mindset as opportunities are seemingly infinite through online resources. The ability to learn virtually anything at any time has allowed for a generation of efficient problem solvers and critical thinkers to excel.

*   *

WORK BALANCE

In many instances they are perceived as Millennial laziness but it can actually be contributed to a greater emphasis on measuring performance by overall impact and output rather than just time spent on it. Focusing on quality of work rather than the hours worked on it has led to a re-imagned work week. We are starting to see less and less of the 40-hour week and commute to work. And honestly, it makes sense for many companies and workers, not all, but many. (Fromm)

An estimated three million Americans work from home, and that number is expected to increase 63 percent over the next five years. According to Pew Research Center, "If they were able to make their current job more flexible, 64 percent of millennials want to occasionally work from home and 66 percent would like to shift their hours."

The most important thing to remember is that the **millennial worker no longer works *for* you; they work *with* you.**

"Creating an environment that aligns with the participation economy will be your biggest opportunity to create a company where millennials not only want to work, but will seek your company out as a top professional career" (Fromm).

*   *

ME: What experience or upbringing led you towards social entrepreneurship and starting something yourself?

ARI: My grandmother the holocaust survivor. She's 94 years old. And she had inspired my entire family to fight for what you believe in. And also to never lose hope. To stay strong at all times and to remember that, you know, there's an inherent goodness to humanity. She is the inspiration to my whole family in particular, we build on that kind of mentality. She had to struggle to just stay alive: living in the ward she weighed 55 pounds. She lost her family. Yet she persevered and ended up having a beautiful family afterwards. I don't know if I'll be able to conquer something of such a great magnitude in my life. But she inspired everyone in her family to do amazing things because, even though it wasn't really about her DNA, my dad, everyone's really been small business owners and entrepreneurs. I come from a family who has done really well over themselves in their own thing. So it's kind of like DNA in a sense with my dad, and my grandmother as well.

On my mom's side, my grandfather was a huge entrepreneur, and again, it's DNA. He inspired me also to just go after it. His whole mentality was, "I'm gonna make it happen." He also taught me: *Tikkun Olam*—it's just making the world a better place. This word has really resonated with me and my family my whole life. My family, who've been literally persecuted because of who they are and what they believe in and yet, despite we've always thought to make the world a better place. So I've been inspired by many people, by my grandmother, she nearly lost her family because of it, and then she went to my grandfather as a result of who she was. It also inspired me to do good the world and how important that is. It's doing what's important to you and making it happen at all costs. So it keeps two things and again really contribute to me being able to do what i do.

I wouldn't be where I am today without that background. Because otherwise that'd just be, you know, I will be just doing a repeat class. Doing what everyone else is doing. Sitting at the back just I wouldn't be fighting for anything particular. I'd be doing my homework then going to class. But you know my family's like, we're gonna be doing something ourselves. We're gonna be doing something that's big and great, and also it's really important to make sure that you're always doing things to better everyone. Not just yourselves.

So I think that's the long answer to your question.

CHAPTER 2

A BRIEF HISTORY OF CORPORATE GIVING

"Dad, can we go back to Woods Hole tomorrow?" I'd asked.

"Why?" He glanced up from his book.

"Remember that shark's tooth necklace I saw? I decided I want to buy it. Can you drive me back and get it for me?"

My dad smiled. It was a classic seven-year-old move that he'd seen before. I'd buried the lead: *Buy it for me.*

He was much too smart for that. My father would teach me a lesson about doing well and giving back that I would never forget.

Before Corporate Philanthropy became integrated into businesses, the leaders and founders of innovative companies were
aligning their values and interests with the success of their
companies. Here in Michigan, I've gone to The Henry Ford
Museum of American Innovation, only 30 minutes away from
campus in Dearborn, Michigan. The museum is a collection of
American Inventions and machinery that Henry Ford believed
in and felt were bridges between the technology of the past
and the technology of the future. Ford wanted to share with
the public his idea of "how far and how fast we have come."
(McClimon) Ford's actions were an early introduction to a
corporation sharing what they believe in, and giving back.

Ford was not the only entrepreneur and innovator of the time
to begin giving back. John Pierpont Morgan, founder of J.P.
Morgan, now JP Morgan Chase, aligned his passion for art
and books with his business, which allowed him to collect
an extensive assortment of works that eventually ended up
in the Metropolitan Museum of Art. Morgan also built his
company on his values of trust, integrity and wealth.

Maggie Lena Walker was the first woman bank president
in the United States, founding St. Luke Penny Savings Bank
in Richmond, Virginia in 1905. She was a firm believer that
African-Americans should put their money back into their

own communities, and the bank's slogan was: "Bring it all back home" (McClimon).

Similarly, Alexander Graham Bell, founder of the Bell Telephone Company (AT&T today), devoted part of his life to teaching lip reading to his wife and others who were impaired. This work, in which he studied waves and transmission of sound, eventually led him to the invention of the telephone.

Myra Bradwell was denied entry into the Illinois Bar Association in 1868, prompting the foundation of The Chicago Legal News, the first major legal journal in the Western U.S. She made sure to include articles on women's issues that directly related to promoting legal reforms for women, especially their right to vote (McClimon).

Each of these men and women were not CEO's—they didn't have that title at the time—but they were leaders who believed in something, and shaped their business around that belief. While it was not at the core of their business model, it influenced the way they conducted business.

*   *

"Tim, how much lemonade have you sold?" my father asked me after my first hour.

"None. Well two glasses, but it was just to mom and you, so that doesn't count."

He could sense my frustration.

After being told I'd need to figure out my own way to get the money for the shark's tooth necklace, I'd been struck by a brilliant idea. The Falmouth Road Race is an annual seven-mile race that happens each August. As luck would have it, the course passed right by the house where we were staying at in the Cape.

"We should clean up the front yard," my grandmother had commented. "There are probably going to be a thousand people or more who walk by it this weekend for the race."

The Light Bulb: A thousand people? Wait a second....

Shark Tooth Necklace...money...tons of people walking by with money...pretty cute kid somehow asking for their money.... "Hmm," I thought. And then it totally lit up, a revolutionary idea hit me!

A Lemonade Stand.

"Perfect," I thought. "Easy to make, easy to sell, everyone loves it." I pitched the idea to the dinner table, and soon enough the whole fam was on board. We began brainstorming about ways to jumpstart my entrepreneurial career, and after five or ten minutes, we had the supplies planned out and the home-made lemonade recipe made up.

I even employed my artistic talents, making a poster that read: "Tim's Lemonade Stand: 50 Cents," with a big lemon under the title. After spending the rest of the night preparing, I went to bed, excited by the prospect of being rich the next day!

The morning rolled around and I set up my table at the end of the driveway at 8 in the morning, laying out a yellow quilted table cover, my huge glass pitcher, and medium sized cups. I strategically placed my table at an angle facing all the walkers headed to the race, with my vibrant poster hanging from the front. It was turning out to be a beautiful morning, at a crisp 75 degrees and heating up; perfect lemonade-craving weather.

But an hour into selling, reality had hit me: sales were dismal.

I was cute, but it seemed there were other enterprising kids earlier on the route who had also set up their own lemonade stands. I was just another kid with freckles hawking lemonade.

"Why do you want the necklace?" my dad asked as I watched another group of walkers pass by.

"I like sharks and a shark's tooth is cool. I dunno."

"Did you know that sharks are often hunted for their fins? And in some places they are becoming endangered."

"Really?"

"Yes, that's one of the reasons why the aquarium has the exhibit about Sharks we saw. Remember it?"

I nodded. Earlier in the summer we'd been to the aquarium and they'd had a huge display of sharks and the dangers of hunting them. It had been my favorite part of that visit, and in some ways was why I decided I needed the necklace.

"How could you help sharks and yourself?" my dad asked.

I paused. "Maybe I could give the aquarium some of the money I make today?"

My dad smiled.

"Okay, but why does that matter? I've only made two dollars anyways."

"Well," my dad said, "maybe people don't know *why* you are selling lemonade and why it matters. Perhaps you need

a better story to tell and that'll help people want to buy
your lemonade."

*   *

A TIMELINE:

In the 1950s the primary focus was on businesses' responsibilities to society and doing good deeds for society.

In the 1960s key events, people and ideas were instrumental in characterizing the social changes ushered in during this decade.

In the 1970s business managers applied the traditional management functions when dealing with CSR issues.

While, in the 1980s, business and social interest came closer and firms became more responsive to their shareholders.

During the 1990s, the idea of CSR became almost universally approved, with CSR being coupled with strategy literature.

And, finally, in the 2000s, CSR definitively became an important strategic issue (Moura-Leite, Padgett).

*   *

My dad came back to my stand with a marker.

"Add that you will be donating half your sales to the local Woods Hole Aquarium," he said. "Add it under the lemon on the poster." I was skeptical, but reluctantly agreed to the idea.

With my new addition to the sign, I sat back in my seat, patiently waiting for the next flow of customers to start strolling by. Then, about fifteen minutes later, my first potential customer wandered by—she was an older lady walking with her husband. Like most people before her, she'd looked at me and the lemonade on my table and smiled. She was wearing big sunglasses and a visor. But then something remarkable happened.

She stopped.

Grabbing her husband's arm and pulling him to my table, she motioned to my poster for a second before smiling and asking me my name.

"My name is Timmy," I said, laying on the charm.

Then she continued as she pulled out her wallet, "Well good morning, Timmy. I have to be honest with you: I did not expect to be buying lemonade this early in the day, but given that it is homemade AND that you are donating to the aquarium I couldn't resist. Why did you decide to give half of your money to the aquarium?"

My dad, who had lingered behind after bringing me the marker, was smirking.

And I wasn't ready for this kind of question since, honestly, it wasn't my idea. Fortunately, I was quick on my feet. I told her, "Well I really like the animals there and want to help them save more of the endangered fish and turtles that I saw the other day, and I also really want to buy a shark tooth necklace I saw on our bike ride yesterday!"

As I shakily poured her glass of lemonade, she smiled and said, "Well I have been going to that aquarium with my grandchildren for the past fifteen years. I love that you're giving back; you are being very thoughtful."

I said thank you with a huge grin on my face, patiently awaiting my first 50 cents, and handed her the cup of lemonade. She took a sip and told me it was perfect, just what she needed. And then, to my absolute amazement, she handed me a 5 dollar bill.

I was in shock!

She proceeded to wish me good luck with my stand, as I reveled over my first five dollar bill, and quickly found a safe spot in my plastic money bag. Soon after, I had customers flooding in as they read my poster (and also to get a refreshing cup of lemonade during the now 90 degrees summer morning).

Now I don't mean to toot my own horn, but my homemade recipe was pretty darn good, so good that people were coming back for seconds. Soon, I had made $50 in four hours—a huge improvement over my first disappointing hour on the course.

I quickly did the math in my 7-year-old head: splitting that would keep $25 for myself, which was enough to buy two necklaces, if I wanted. And I could donate a lot of money to the aquarium.

I ran up to my dad, holding my 50 dollars. My dad, being the good father that he is, was proud of me, but had another learning lesson in mind. Of course I had to learn that day that there's this thing called a savings account, and its supposedly a smart idea to start saving early. So I reluctantly agreed to put $10 of my $25 to my savings, meaning I could still buy the necklace, but it would no longer be 'raining shark teeth.'

*   *

Humans are emotional creatures. And while our parents' generation might call millennials soft, and coddled, in reality, this generation is possibly the most emotionally-driven generation to ever promote change in our society, the environment, and in the workplace. And businesses are tapping into this emotion by believing in the same things as their consumer. I am living this perspective and I find myself buying new products every other week, products that go the extra mile to align with things I care about, just as my customers bought my lemonade. I have engaged with countless other students and friends and had conversations about the changes they want to see in the world. Many of these have to do with alleviating Poverty, Climate Change, and World Health and how companies that have an impact on issues like these, that create meaningful change, and care about what they do, stand out amongst the rest of the competition.

I've talked to innovators and leaders who have tapped into this different frame of reference as well, and have seen the effect it's had on their businesses. In the words of Priya Bery, Ex VP of Social Entrepreneurship at TOMS, "…my passion and excitement stemmed from and the taking a business approach in addressing issues such as World Health, was not to make money off of it but to attempt incredible solutions that may not have been realized otherwise because of this different channel of resources and people. And so it was really the first steps of blurring the lines between the public sector, private sector, and the social sector so that accessing all of that can create all kind of good. Supporting the idea that it can be very possible and ethical to be making money and doing good at the same time. And there are some that do it better than others, and some that are more ethical about it. And when you find a business that do it right at their core you than its real.

Take this into account: "Millennials, on average, are more risk-averse and are less likely to spend money unnecessarily than previous generations. But when millennials do decide to part with their money, key patterns are emerging. Millennials prefer to do business with corporations and brands with pro-social messages, sustainable manufacturing methods and ethical business standards." (Landrum)

And it has taken many companies a long time to come around to this new market, but what it really comes back to is the very simple concept laid out by Simon Sinek: that people, and millennials in particular, don't buy what you do, they buy WHY you do it.

* *

That afternoon, my dad took me to the store, where I settled on a medium sized hammerhead tooth with two green beads on either side. $10 was a bargain for that beauty, plus I still had $5 to spare.

I was still rich.

Our next stop would be the aquarium, where I'd donate the other half of my haul. We locked our bikes outside and walked in, passing the seal swimming pool in the front where a huge crowd had gathered to watch the seals train their tricks. I had already seen the show three times, so we walked right in and went over to the front desk.

"Can I help you gentlemen with anything?" the lady sitting at the front desk asked us.

"Nope," I replied. "I'm just here to make a donation to the aquarium."

My dad smiled. Charm must run in the family.

"Well, aren't you quite the philanthropist," she replied. "Why did you decide to make a donation to our aquarium today?"

I shared the entire story—including the last minute modification to the poster and its impact on my success. Then I proudly showed off my shark tooth necklace. The woman beamed as she listened to my story, and as soon as I'd finished up, made a quick call.

"Someone will be right up to meet you," she said to me as she hung up the phone.

Soon a staff member a light blue shirt, khaki shorts, and hiking shoes met my dad and I at the desk. I extended my small hand with the money and again retold my story without leaving out a single detail.

"The aquarium thanks you for giving back," she said with a smile. Then, looking at my father before looking back at me, she said, "We'd like to give something back to you."

She told my dad and I to follow her down to a door that read, EMPLOYEES ONLY. I was getting super excited as she told us they don't usually let anyone in this part of the aquarium where they keep the rescued sea life. We turned the corner and came up to a tank where she showed me the four endangered turtles they had rescued the week before. I stared down at the turtles in awe, amazed that they could be so endangered.

I'd received a *private* tour of the lab, been able to see four rescue turtles up close *and* had my necklace. This was turning into quite the day.

I definitely was no longer salty about the $25 I'd donated. I walked out of the aquarium with a deep sense of fulfillment, and at 7 years old I didn't really know why I felt like that, but in retrospect, I had learned a very important aspect of business. I learned that business happens on a personal level. I learned that people wanted to buy my lemonade, not just

because it tasted amazing, but because it had a purpose—
there was a reason I was selling it.

Young Timmy didn't quite realize his first business was a
Corporate Mission Model, but in fact, it had been (I guess
father's do know a thing or two).

*   *

How will the Corporate Mission Model change CSR? Well in
many ways it already has, but much of that change is being
driven by the very customers that now represent the largest
portion of the workforce: the youth.

Today, business has the power to bring purpose to people's
lives. It is not the corporate-dominated world of our parents'
and parents' parents' generation where we are going to work
long, dry hours at companies driven only by profit. It is not a
world where capitalism is hated for its skew. It's becoming clear
that harnessing the power, organization, profit, and purpose
of companies in order to create meaningful, long-term change
in all sectors of society is imperative when it comes to solving the biggest problems we face today. We can no longer be
driven by impersonal and indirect business, dominated by
short term gains and disregard for what we take out of the
environment and society.

And we are seeing change, short-term and long-term, with the help of a generation of mindful millennials, who are itching for change, and desire to see a world that can sustain itself through an economy that is profitable, socially-conscious, and effective. Millennials are demanding these changes in the workplace, in education systems, from their government, and from the businesses from whom they purchase goods and services. And the organizations that respond to these demands are taking off; they're not only profitable, they are stable, transparent, and inspiring to their consumers.

CHAPTER 3

CORPORATE MISSION MODEL

———

When I began recruiting for a full-time job the summer before my senior year of college, I told a successful businessman and philanthropist that I wanted a job that was so mission-driven and fulfilling that "work never felt like work." He told me, "work will always feel like work and you have to build an established career before you can be mission-driven and give back." Thank you to the company and the people who have proven him wrong. Not a morning person, I wake up amped every single day to go to "work" and feel fulfilled on a personal and macro level. Immensely grateful in this reflective season for each coworker and my incredible leadership team.

—AN "UNSETTLER"—EVA SCARANO,
UNIVERSITY OF MICHIGAN '17

Eva is an Unsettler. She didn't let one person stuck in their ways tell her that her definition of happiness and purpose in her job and in a corporation didn't exist. Because it does. And it's manifested itself as a model for the best and brightest companies today that want to attract the top talent and the most passionate people who will help build their tribe.

While this model is never simple and does not apply to every company the same way, there are certain features of any Corporate Mission Model that are essential to creating the culture of doing well by doing good. Follow along to learn how to build yours.

*　*

BUILD YOUR TRIBE

A tribe is a group if people connected to one another, connected to a leader, and connected to an idea (Sivers). A tribe consists of inspired employees, of passionate, relentless leaders, a mission, and an emphasis on challenging the status quo. But this is leadership beyond hierarchy. It has very little to do with management level. These are things that drive profit, and change.

Our flexibility in who we 'follow' and how we challenge the constructs around us is often portrayed as signs of disrespect for authority, hierarchy or tradition. But from my perspective, the truth is that we just don't automatically associate these terms with leadership.

We lead, learn from, and openly challenge the status quo around us—regardless of where we fall on the corporate ladder. The benefits of this are self-evident to us millennials. We're not sure why it isn't to everyone else.

Be transparent and authentic.

—RENÉE WALKOM, MBA, GLOBALLY MINDED
HR AND TALENT MANAGEMENT PROFESSIONAL

Millennials want to learn. They want to learn from leaders who are accessible and who create direction. A major reason that millennials are likely to leave their current job is actually because of their boss. It's vital that a leader creates an environment where all employees, including millennials, feel supported and valued. It leads to increased productivity and valuable relationships. And this means the relationship between the employee and supervisor needs to extend further than the annual check-in or work review.

In a recent study by TriNet, a company dedicated to providing HR solutions, sixty-nine percent of millennials see their company's review process as flawed. A major source of this is that millennial employees don't feel like they are given enough feedback about their performance. The study finds that seventy-five percent millennials feel this way, and ninety percent of millennials would feel more confident if they had more frequent meetings and evaluations with their boss. (Bellis)

"The biggest issue with the annual review process is the formality. There is often more emphasis on reflection rather than opportunities for improvement in the future," said Rob Hernandez, Perform Product Manager at TriNet.

The relationship needs to move away from the formality and start focusing on improvement, and it needs to start from the leadership position. For an employee that wants to learn, you are more than their boss: you are their coach. And the best leaders of the best and most companies all share certain qualities that inspire their tribe and sees their mission to fruition. These leaders have a cause worth fight for with an irresistible call to action that inspires and drives commitment. They don't water down their message to please everyone. They Enable followers to be connected and constantly challenge the status quo. They find other leaders, amplify their work, and help them find followers. And they shine light on their tribe.

*   *

DEFINE THE PROBLEM YOU ARE SOLVING

"If I were given one hour to save the planet, I would spend 59 minutes defining the problem and one minute resolving it," Albert Einstein said.

Trying to solve a problem without knowing exactly what it is is a pitfall into which any organization (or leader) may fall. Especially when developing new products, processes, or even businesses, most companies do not spend the time or resources in defining the full scope and scale of whatever problem they are trying to solve. Once again, leadership is essential in this position, as articulating the problem requires a full understanding of all of its aspects, as well as a full understanding of why solving this particular problem is important. Without this kind of leadership or commitment to this development, companies and organizations miss opportunities and waste resources.

No matter if you are a product genius, a Forbes "30 Under 30," or have the financial savvy of Warren Buffet, at the end of the day, your success as a business leader or entrepreneur is predicated by how well you can define and solve problems, whether they are big problems, little problems, global problems, or even First-world problems says Thomas Oppong, young entrepreneur and Founder of Alltopstartups.

So no matter what problem you solve, solve problems that matter.

*   *

SCALE

Scale is possibly one of the most important ideas moving forward in business. It is something that Ari stressed in our conversation about GiveButter, where learning to be successful on a small scale, is crucial to being confident in having a similar impact as you grow.

When thinking holistically about building your business, remember that a company's outcomes are also affected by the larger ecosystem around that business, an ecosystem filled with numerous other participants. These participants can include sales clerks, suppliers, industry regulators, competitors, even delivery drivers. A successful business must think holistically about how best to serve the needs of its customers within the context of this larger system.

Michael Porter, a renowned business professor at Harvard Business School, expands this idea: "The ultimate impact businesses can have is through the business itself. There are huge unmet needs in the world today. The question now is how to get capitalism to operate at its best because capitalism is fundamentally the best way to meet needs. If you can meet needs at a profit, you can scale" (Schiller).

Two things need to be taken into account when building on this success: short-term and long-term growth. Business is experiencing exponential change in this perfect storm, but in this short-term growth and change there is a need to build for a future, to think-long term, to think beyond the boundary of profit and build a solid foundation and team. When growing this core team there is a balance to be struck with establishing a model of gradual expansion at an intentional rate, yet there can be no hesitation to invest and grow staff.

Fagan Harris, CEO and President of Baltimore Corps, lays out that, "One of the most important lessons we learned in the early-goings of our organization's life cycle was that our team is the single greatest investment we can make in our future—that the expansion of our core team doesn't depend on the capacity we've built, but rather our ability to expand our capacity depends on the contributors we add. There will likely be times when you don't feel ready to make the leap, but it may be the most important thing your organization can do" (Yu).

Additionally, an early top priority for entrepreneurs is to quickly define a target customer and client. Ari and his team knew their target was college students, and the company has flourished on the enthusiastic response from them. In Ari's case, college students were lined up to benefit the most from GiveButter, and Ari's close focus on the customer and the customer experience animates the social entrepreneur as much as it does the business entrepreneur. Each gets out of bed every day to serve a purpose, to change the equilibrium for a defined population. Social entrepreneurs aim to make a difference for someone in particular and build off that impact.

The Key Investment to Scale is Mentorship and Network. Experienced people create an echo chamber of growth, and a network to which you can always turn for guidance and wisdom.

*   *

Take some notes on David Foster and Sam Polk's scaling methods in the development of their L.A. based company, Everytable, a healthy and affordable alternative to rival the fast food industry. **The scale of the need:** look at a map of L.A. and every source of healthy food exists only in wealthier areas.

- **The scale of the opportunity:** look at a map of L.A., and every fast food chain you can think of exists in huge numbers in poorer areas.
- **The smarts of the team:** Sam and David were former finance guys and had a knack for analyzing this problem and coming

up with an innovative new solution. They understood the economics of fast food chain models and they took the best from those models and improved upon them with healthy ingredients and appropriate pricing depending on the neighborhood (Enso).

Foster and Polk continue to grow Everytable, and have the ambitious goal to scale from California communities to other communities in the U.S., with a weather eye on the global horizon. They kept their mission simple and authentic. Regardless of how many advertising dollars a company spends, the aim isn't to sell a product, but, rather, to establish a relationship with the community. The irony is that when a company shifts its focus away from selling, it will typically sell more.

*　*

STORIES BUILD THE BRAND

Your company is a story before it is a brand. Its beginning had to come from something. Your brand is built by the people that believe in your story, be it your customers, employees, or investors. It is vital to be clear and authentic in why you do what you do, and use your company's story as your marketing tool. What you'll find is that companies that do this right end up spending little to no money on marketing campaigns. Their story becomes their brand, and it's shared by millions.

So how do you share your story? Publish a book? Hand out pamphlets to every customer? Rent dozens of billboards in every city in America, telling your story serially, like a television show? Here are some tips from Zachary Quinn and Brian Keller, co-founders of Love Your Melon, A Minnesota Startup that Scaled To $40 Million Selling U.S.-Manufactured Clothing. Part of the reason they achieved this profit—perhaps the only reason—is because they used their company's story to cut marketing costs close to zero.

CREATE GOOD CONTENT

"Quality eats everything else, especially in this day and age," Quinn says. "They see so much, and their attention spans are so short." If you don't invest in quality, you might as well flush your money down the toilet. "We do five photoshoots a week all around the country, which turns into content for social media and advertising." A third of the employees work on the manufacturing; a third work on operations, and a third work in marketing—which is mostly the content creation (MacBride).

EXPERIMENT AND SHIFT, CONSTANTLY

Consumer tastes change. High-quality photographs have been powerful for a while, but now Love Your Melon is shifting a portion of its resources to video. "We've found the most effective is six-second videos," Quinn said. But the secret isn't any specific medium; it's being in tune to your customers' tastes. So the content Love Your Melon creates might be about an event at a local restaurant, or a post about one of its college ambassadors on a trip. There are so many different social media outlets out there today, and it's completely free to post on them. Using your company's story in short video bits and creating a relationship with an evolving customer base is crucial (MacBride).

DO IT YOURSELF

Quinn also advises against hiring a marketing agency. In the rapidly changing world of social media, "nobody knows what they're doing," he said. It takes more time to coordinate an outside agency than it's worth; his inside team, which is immersed in the company's culture, can do the same work by experimenting (MacBride).

*   *

INNOVATE YOUR MODEL BY CREATING SMART PARTNERSHIPS

The best for-profit social enterprises that have been success-ful have used a variety of business models, each with a similar motive, yet each goes about it differently than the others. Here are some of the ways the top mission-based companies have used smart partnerships in innovative ways:

SUPPLY CHAIN

Companies are building NGOs and Non-Profits into the supply chain by looking at everything from the ingredients, materials, and operations, to the workers and practices. Map out your chain and keep it transparent; show how the product gets to the consumer, and the ripple it makes on its way there. Some of the most serious problems are being tackled by the cooperation between for-profit supply chain models and NGOs and Non-Profits. Innovative companies are setting up supply chains in ways that give work to people and, in the process, are educating them, giving them food to eat (thus helping alleviate malnutrition), giving work and hope to people caught in human trafficking, and so forth. In the end though, businesses are using this model to give people purpose and meaningful work.

Here's how NGOs and Non-Profits are playing three distinct new roles in partnership with corporations:

INNOVATION PARTNERS

Many established NGOs and Non-Profits have decades of

experience working with under-served communities and, therefore, are a contextual database of knowledge and cultural awareness. They've developed trusted relationships that are often difficult for private companies to create, especially companies who usually look to develop quickly and bypass creating valuable relationships. NGOs and Non-Profits are masters of specialized knowledge, allowing companies to tailor their product or service to a specific target population and market. A prime example of this is Save the Children, who helps GlaxoSmithKline by serving on the company's new pediatric research and development board. Their mission: to help design life-saving drugs for children in remote communities (Mahmud).

EXPERT GIVERS

NGO's and Non-Profits have an expertise in service delivery. This wouldn't sound very important at first, yet in my interview with Priya Bery who worked closely with TOMS CEO and Chief Giver, Blake Mycoskie, she highlighted that, "If he was on the call right now he'd tell you that **giving is harder than selling** and he had no idea when he started the company."

Giving the right way is hard. NGOs' and Non-Profits' expertise allows them to carry out direct interventions with individuals and local organizations more efficiently than the private sector. For example, TechnoServe has utilized their partnership with

Nespresso to efficiently and intimately offer training and capacity building to coffee farmers in East Africa. "This training helps the company maintain the quality and consistency of its supply chain and increases the income of local farmers at the same time" (Mahmud). Corporations and NGOs and Non-Profits need to jointly identify such common goals and the companies that can articulate this goal and create these partnerships at the core of their business are the ones that create meaningful change in the lives of millions.

STRATEGIC ADVISORS

NGOs and Non-Profits have an extensive knowledge on such topics as climate change, financial access and *last mile delivery* (a term used in supply chain management and transportation planning to describe the movement of people and goods from a transportation hub to a final destination in the home. This knowledge comes, largely, from the Public Sector.

The public sector is a valuable advisor in assessing community needs, understanding policy implications and identifying customized solutions for specific contexts and target populations. Mixing this kind of expertise with the efficiency and resources of corporations is a valuable connection that has been lacking in industries across the board. With the high-level organization and discipline of the private sector, NGOs and Non-Profits are also provided the tools to create new and innovative tools to further advance their mission and their corporate partnerships.

The World Wildlife Fund has helped Coca-Cola develop models and create a framework to evaluate tradeoffs between conserving biodiversity and minimizing costs. The partnership has resulted in improved ecological health of seven of the world's most important freshwater basins, while improving Coca-Cola's water efficiency by more than 20% (Mahmud).

SHARED VALUE

Shared value is not the answer to all the worlds problems, but it's been a valuable stepping stone towards creating effective partnerships that help companies understand the problem they are trying to solve, articulate it, and identify the specific intersections of social challenges. This full understanding of their business constraints and opportunities opens the door to determine the gaps in their assets that NGO and Non-Profit partners can fill.

This is not simple philanthropy. This is real change. And it's where leadership is crucial to either guide this initiative, or bring in senior leadership that can quickly mobilize this type of initiative. But when done well, wow, these partnerships create spectacular opportunities for businesses to access new and developing markets, to be more efficient, and to change people's lives.

One more example of a company that is really on-board with this is, Cotopaxi, who has partnered with **five** different non-profits throughout their supply chain and business model. They support what Smith calls "The Three Pillars," pillars that support a pathway out of poverty: health, education, and livelihoods

These five organizations include:

- Educate Girls—India
- Fundación Escuela Nueva—Latin America
- Proximity Designs—Myanmar
- International Rescue Committee—Middle East and Europe
- Nothing But Nets—Sub-Saharan Africa

In addition to working with these non-profits, Cotopaxi goes beyond these partnerships by working closely with local communities to preserve the tradition of llama farming. This creates pathways to market for rural smallholder farmers who would otherwise make less than $100 a year! Cotopaxi's Kusa Collection utilizes the natural insulating fiber from llamas raised from these very remote parts of the Altiplano, Bolivia's high desert (Smith).

In addition, theDel Dia line of backpacks are manufactured in the Philippines, where the company provides fair wages and hours. More than that, though, the people who sew together Cotopaxi's expedition-level backpacks are given the opportunity to participate in the design process, instead of simply being told what to do. So most of them add their own custom stitching, pockets, or customized design accents. And the high quality fabrics used for these backpacks are actually the recycled waste fabrics from factories. Cotopaxi has demonstrated that there are endless ways to approach sustainable and impactful work.

"Our customers love the creative uniqueness of each of our backpacks," says Smith, "and the people we work with love feeling that they're involved in creating something that becomes a personal piece of art. If you start thinking about people throughout your entire product process as a core value, these are the little things that emerge that can change your company's entire approach to design and development" (Lane Taylor).

The Corporate Mission Model is simple:

- Build Your Tribe
- Define the Problem You are Solving
- Learn to Scale
- Use Your Story
- Innovate Your Model by Creating Smart Partnerships

Throughout my research and conversations, the Corporate Mission Model I've laid out highlights the most important actions a company can take to align its business with its purpose. Throughout the rest of this book, you will continue to learn how to use business to solve problems that matter and, at the same time, create a company that gives back to society in a meaningful ways.

CHAPTER 4

INVESTING IN IMPACT

In the past two decades, Governments, Charity organizations, non-profits, and CSR programs have all addressed different social issues pressing our society such as poverty, health and disease, and lack of educational. Yet they all work within their own sectors and are therefore limited in their impact. They are stuck in an age-old way of approaching and solving problems.

"Interviews conducted in 2000 by the Social Investment Task Force in the United Kingdom, revealed what most nonprofit leaders already know: Almost all social sector organizations are small and perennially underfunded, with barely three months' worth of working capital at their disposal. And that hasn't changed in the last 12 years" (Sir Ronald Cohen and William A. Sahlman).

The old way of doing things is being passed by social entrepreneurs and large companies with stable funding and the innate ability to innovate. Yet traditional forms of funding are a roadblock to scaling the impact of these companies as they have a difficult time finding access to capital markets. With little flexibility in funding, it is hard for companies to grow and experiment at different stages of growth.

Yet, we are most likely on the threshold of a major change, one that reflects the early days of the modern venture capital industry. Venture capital emerged as a machine of professionally managed venture capital partnerships after the 60's ad 70's. These relationships and organizational methods allowed for a huge inflow of capital, and became a core part of driving economics forward (Sir Ronald Cohen and William A. Sahlman).

It changed entrepreneurship.

Impact investing is a way of investing that generates both a positive social impact as well as a return on capital. Like CSR, it merges the old dichotomy, the binary view that businesses were for profit, and charities were for social change. But it also goes a step further.

Impact investment sets out to harness the power of business and use it to tackle social challenges. One example of this is d.light, a company that produces low-cost solar lighting for poorer areas. Currently, d.light produces half a million solar lanterns every month. They are already providing safe and reliable lighting to over 20 million people worldwide and aim to increase this number five-fold by 2020 (Mahmud).

Businesses that provide low-cost but innovative goods and services for the poor, such as solar lighting, can sometimes be seen as too risky by traditional investors. But risk-taking impact investors have given d.light the opportunity to prove its business case, transforming itself from a small-scale operation to a thriving global enterprise.

"We are in the early days of an important shift, similar in impact to the rise of the modern venture capital industry fifty years ago. The rise of venture capital led to whole new types of investment models for entrepreneurs, helping to transform economies and boost prosperity. We are seeing start-ups and innovative products pop up around the world, not just in Silicon Valley and London, but in Nairobi, Delhi and Lagos," says Sir Ronald Cohen, also known as the father of social investment.

The business world is not the sector recognizing this important trend, as various governments are also encouraging this type of investment. David Cameron, Previous Prime Minister of England, reiterated in a speech at the Social Impact Investment

Forum in London, "We've got a great idea here that can transform our societies, by using the power of finance to tackle the most difficult social problems. Problems that have frustrated government after government, country after country, generation after generation. Issues like drug abuse, youth unemployment, homelessness and even global poverty. The potential for social investment is that big" (Gov.UK).

"More than 300 investment professionals from across the planet gathered in London at a forum organized by the Global Impact Investing Network (GIIN). They included senior figures from some of the world's leading financial institutions, as well as representatives from philanthropic investment firms and foundations. GIIN believes that what we invest in today will determine the world we live in tomorrow, and this group is playing a leading role in addressing global challenges, using impact investing to complement public resources and philanthropy" (Mahmud).

Yet there are still many challenges ahead. "Venture capital took decades to become truly viable, and the impact investing industry will not mature overnight. To reach scale, impact investors will need to continue to take high risks on new business ideas and—just like venture capital—see lots of failures scattered among an emerging landscape of breakthrough successes. In time, impact investing will solidify itself and become the greatest catalyst for change and long-term

sustainable social and highly profitable business that our society has been chasing" (Mahmud).

Many valuable lessons have already been learned as the first generation of impact investing focused on initiatives that would deliver the greatest financial and social returns. While this approach was undeniably instrumental in helping to make the case for impact investing, it meant that strategic investments in varied stages of development of companies were overlooked. As the blueprint of a successful, and highly profitable social enterprise becomes more methodical, the timing and success rate of investment become more efficient and profitable. Investors are able to meet the acute need to invest in the early stages of innovation, creating capital for a rapid scale-up and breakthrough onto the commercial scene.

The drawbacks are familiar, but surmountable over time. As the first iteration of impact investing focused on initiatives that would benefit everyone both socially and financially, important lessons were learned. Most notably, we learned how to better invest and innovate in the earliest stages of development. And, of course, as we learn, our procedures become more practiced, allowing for more investment, more innovation, more capital and, ultimately, a more rapid upward scale.

*　*

"Today it's hard to imagine what our world would be like without the many innovations catalyzed by venture capital, from the commercial internet to the mobile phone" (Mahmud).

Paula Goldman, senior director of knowledge and advocacy at Omidyar Network, believes that, "Fifteen years from now...we'll say the same about impact investing. We'll look back on a host of innovations benefitting millions of disadvantaged people—in education, in healthcare, and yes, in solar lighting—and will have a hard time remembering the day when people viewed charity and business as working towards opposite goals."

Society is going to experience a new round of change in the next five to ten years when investors ride the same wave of courage they surfed in the early stages of development in the venture capital industry. We are going to see talented, purpose-driven social entrepreneurs build large, effective organizations that disrupt social issues at their core and deliver huge profits at the same time.

CHAPTER 5

SELL STORIES, NOT PRODUCTS

Today's most successful businesses are built on their story.

Companies with stories at their core beyond just creating a narrative around which to market their business. Their story shines through their products or service in all aspects and through every action. And it is *action*, not *advertising*, that makes them successful. The best-run companies, all the way from small startups to huge corporations, manifest everything—from product design to customer service to marketing—around their story (Montague).

THE SCIENCE OF STORIES

Stories have been around for a *very* long time. Cavemen told the first stories on the walls of caves. Today, we post "stories" all the time on snapchat, or use a story to explain a crazy night out to one of our friends. We all enjoy a good story; it captivates us (Wildrich).

If you're sitting in a big lecture hall listening to a professor lecture from slides with bullet points and quick blurbs of information, only a few certain parts of your brain are activated to soak in that information. Scientists call these parts Broca's area and Wernicke's area (Wildrich).

But, when I'm sitting around a bonfire at home after getting back from school with my high school buddies listening to their crazy stories from school things change dramatically. Not only is the language processing parts of my brain activated, but any other part of my brain that I would have used to experience the events of my friends story is also firing off.

A story gets your whole brain working; it's like fireworks in your head. And it's quite a show.

What's even crazier is that, "When we tell stories to others that have helped us shape our thinking and way of life, we can have the same effect on them too. The brains of the person telling a story and listening to it, can synchronize," says Uri Hasson from Princeton.

When you tell a story that people believe in, that people want to experience for themselves, your frontal cortex is going 100 mph, and for the people listening, their frontal cortex are lighting up too, not literally, but like the fireworks. And guess what our frontal cortex does? It's the control panel of our personality and our ability to communicate, and so there is a science behind storytelling.

*   *

Take Davis and Asialene Smith's story, for example. When they founded Cotopaxi, they were very serious about making a difference in the world. It is the fulfillment of Smith's desire to help people, a desire that began when he was a little boy.

When Smith was a toddler, his father's job supervising construction for The Church of Jesus Christ of Latter-day Saints took his family to the Dominican Republic, Puerto Rico and Ecuador. For Smith, this meant adventures with his dad, like building their own raft and fishing for piranhas while floating down the Amazon River, or camping on an uninhabited island, surviving off fish they had caught themselves... with spears.

But it also meant being exposed to extreme poverty.

"Some of my earliest memories…are seeing children my age, 3 or 4 years old, that were completely naked on the sides of the street, and you can't have that experience as a child and not have it shape who you are."

His time abroad instilled in Smith a desire to help people, and after returning from a mission in Bolivia, Smith read an article about a man named Steve Gibson. The article told of Gibson's success as an entrepreneur, but it also told of how Gibson and wife, Bette, founded the Academy, a school designed to help returned missionaries learn how to start and grow a business.

Smith cut the article out and put it in the front of his binder where he would see it many times throughout the day. According to Smith, a chance encounter with Gibson on the BYU campus during a social impact conference led to his decision to become an entrepreneur as a means of making an impact on the world.

Guess what Smith did next.

In an interview from Cotopaxi's Facebook page, Smith and his wife recount the story of a street boy named Edgar that sparked the Do Good mentality behind their business. "In 2001, my wife and I were newlyweds and we decided that we wanted to have an adventure together so we found this unpaid internship in Peru and we decided to do it together so we went off to Lima and spent some time there. During this time we decided to go up to Macchu Picchu and flew into Cusco, the city next to it.

When you get there, the first place you go is the main plaza. Right when you walk into the main plaza, there's street children everywhere. They're always looking to approach you and sell you finger puppets or jewelry or postcards or to shine your shoes. We unexpectedly befriended a little a little street kid—a kid that shined shoes. He was so desperate to shine Davis's shoes, and he just stuck out to them. I had tennis shoes on, but he was so insistent that he wanted to shine my shoes. Davis and his wife gave him what little money {they} had, and you could tell that he felt better. After doing something kind like that and seeing that type of reaction, you know that you want to keep doing it. It was our last night in Cusco, and as we were walking back to hotel we saw two little boys huddled against each other on the side of the street…my wife recognized one of the little boys as our friend Edgar. We had to wake him up and we were so shocked to see him out that late. I could see on his face that he'd been crying and he told me that his shoe shining kit had been stolen earlier that day and that he was afraid to go home

It was just a heartbreaking thing to see this this poor little kid going through this experience. The next day as I sat on a bus waiting to go to the airport, I saw Edgar running up to the bus. I opened the window just in time to say goodbye to him as we drove away. He ran next to the bus, waving and smiling, with his other hand tightly gripping a large bag of candy he had bought to sell on the streets.

And in fact I've been telling this story since 2001, telling people about Edgar and this experience we had. After that we knew, in our married life, we wanted to help disadvantaged children in other countries Just because of where they were born geographically in the world, they have incredibly difficult lives and it doesn't take much to impact them. You know, it's not too late for other children; there are other children, like Edgar, that we can help in a real way, help impact their lives. Cotopaxi is about finding a way we can sustainably give back to the world" (Smith).

Cotopaxi may be the first ever public benefit corporation to raise venture capital. Others have raised funding from investment firms and introduced this distinction after the fact, but Smith, despite his attorney's pragmatism, set out to raise money from institutional and angel investors who shared his vision (Sarumi).

Among the impressive investor list, he tapped the co-founders of Warby Parker and Harry's, whom were his classmates at

the University of Pennsylvania Wharton School. The founders had approached Smith with the idea of what has become
a beloved glasses brand and sought operational insights from
his previous business. He liked their idea so much that he
made an investment and it's an interesting story arch that
they can now show their commitment to Cotapaxi's success by
investing and sharing their domain knowledge of the impact-
driven business model (Sarumi).

*　*

METASTORY

One of the other core attributes of storydoing companies
is that they have a more clearly defined purpose than other
companies, something that transcends" marketing, advertising, and business itself. And it speaks to other people's
purposes (Montague).

We've discussed the science behind stories, but being aware
of the society we live in today, we can see that we don't all tell
stories the same way. It's no longer just sitting at the dinner
table, or around a fire sharing our favorite memories.

Today, we document a significant portion of our lives on social
media. All of our actions that we display on platforms like
facebook, twitter, snapchat, and instagram contribute to the

way we want to be seen and the thing we want people to know about us. We are actively telling a story every day. We call this our metastory.

A metastory is the story you tell by what you do—how you act. Companies, like people, all have metastories, but—and this is key—a person may, with his or her own metastory, invest into a company's metastory, thereby intertwining the two.

"Stories live in the hearts of human beings and in the future, should be at the core of every business. The truth is you have the power to become an agent of change in your own organization today. You just have to roll up your sleeves and get to work" (Montague).

*   *

PUTTING THIS IN ACTION

Do it right, and you'll put building blocks in place that allow you to develop a thriving brand with an equally thriving future, one that people buy from simply because they love what you do, what you stand for, and the stories you share.

How to invest in your company's story:

Be 100% honest and genuine, 100% of the time. Integrity matters, not only to a company's brand, but to its employees and, most importantly, its consumers. You need a chief story-teller. It might be your leader, a founder, or someone in your tribe that can share the story of your company with passion. But it doesn't stop with the company. It is essential that your storyteller continues to share stories and milestones with consumers, fostering relationships and letting the consumer follow along and grow with you.

Teach the stories to your tribe. "Employees, business partners and customers can co-create meaningful and inspiring stories by developing a shared vision. The key to success in a networked world is to adopt a collaborative storytelling framework"(Sarumi).

In addition to a separate website, tab, or blog devoted to telling the company's story, make sure to use rich, interactive content, including videos, milestones, interviews, and other mediums to share. It will make your story powerful and easy to share.

Keep the stories simple and meaningful. Using simple language is the best way to activate the brain regions that make us truly relate to the situations and happenings in the story.

And remember, as humans, we are here to find meaning. We are also here to help others find that meaning in their lives and in the things they do. Everything else comes secondary to that "why." We want to believe in ourselves and in the notion that we are here for a reason. We want people, companies and products in our lives that make it easier to do so. That is human nature. And so to market something to believe in … that is infinite.

CHAPTER 6

SOLVE PROBLEMS THAT MATTER

—

A single event can awaken within us a stranger totally unknown to us. To live is to be slowly born.

Scott Harrison is the CEO of Charity: Water. His and his company's story has built the foundation for solving a problem that matters to millions, water.

In 2004, a lost and desperately unhappy Scott Harrison left the high-rolling New York City lifestyle for the shores of West Africa. He was leaving behind a lucrative career in the Big Apple, a career of promoting top nightclubs and fashion events, which also promoted a pretty selfish and arrogant way of life for himself. Harrison was facing a spiritual bankruptcy, as he called it, and needed a change. So, in an attempt to revive his lost Christian faith and spirituality, he did something completely opposite of what he had been doing for years: Harrison signed up to volunteer on the MERCY SHIPS, floating hospitals that provided free medical care in the world's poorest nations. The MERCY SHIPS have an extensive 25-year track record of changing lives, and yet many people, including Scott Harrison at the time, have never heard of them.

In his first few weeks with the humanitarian organization, Harrison found himself surrounded by remarkable people who had left their practices and comfortable lives at home to perform operations on thousands of people in need who would otherwise have no access to medical care. These were top doctors and surgeons who were volunteering their time, time for which they could be getting paid.

Harrison's job was the ship's photojournalist, and he quickly understood the same sacrifice the doctors and surgeons had made. Transitioning from his spacious midtown loft for a 150-square-foot cabin with bunk beds, roommates and cockroaches, Harrison had sacrificed much. Fancy restaurants were replaced by a mess hall, feeding 400+ people, army style. He was, at first, uncomfortable with the sudden fall from glory and lavish living, yet, even his 150-square-foot cabin was a blessing when compared to the environment he witnessed through his camera lens. The paralyzing poverty that consumed the lives of millions drew tears from Harrison's eyes as he documented the lives and suffering of so many. Afterwards, once he had settled back on land—now living in Liberia—he found a newly-defined sense of "lavish": a bed, clean running water, and food in his stomach.

Harrison found a special connection to Liberia. The country has no public electricity, running water, or sewage. Harrison spent time putting faces to the world's 1.2 billion living in poverty, many of them living on less that $365 a year. To put that into perspective, Harrison would spend more than that on a bottle of Grey Goose. In one night.

The medical care was determined by patient screenings, where thousands would line up to be seen. They were suffering from enormous, suffocating tumors, cleft lips, and faces eaten by bacteria from water-borne diseases. Many of the conditions are actually prevalent in the west, as well, but when cared for early on, could never progress to the stages that the people lined up were enduring. Watching these patients who were enduring slow, painful deaths, Harrison learned the true meaning of courage. It was this experience—and its impact on him—that led to the birth of his near-obsession with Charity.

Harrison believes that charity is practical. And while it can be difficult, it's always necessary. In Harrison's words:

Charity is the ability to use one's position of influence, relative wealth and power to affect lives for the better. Charity is singular and achievable. There's a biblical parable about a man beaten near death by robbers. He's stripped naked and lying roadside. Most people pass him by, but one man stops. He picks him up and bandages his wounds. He puts him on his horse and walks alongside until they reach an inn. He checks him in and throws down his Amex. Whatever he needs until he gets better. Because he could. (Harrison)

Can you?

*　*

The federal government does not have the flexibility to address many forms of injustice like they could three generations ago. The problems today have grown increasingly complex, and we need to reorganize the problem-solving network that is in place in order to make it more responsive, and with a greater ability to scale. Our societal challenges—in education, health, or the environment—require innovation from all directions, converging into solutions that are both profitable and effective. Business has the unique power to quickly find, elicit, and harness the talent of millions of potential change-makers (Bornstein). Michael Porter, a University Professor at Harvard Business School, who leads the Institute on Strategy and Competitiveness supports this idea as well. His group is dedicated to studying the ways in which competitiveness in both companies and nations can be harnessed as a solution to social problems.

Fortune magazine calls Michael Porter, simply, "The most famous and influential business professor who has ever lived."

He's made a case for letting business solve social problem.

Michael Porter has seen a couple things in how we approach problems that matter in society. We've tended to use NGO's and Non-Profits, turning to the government and philanthropy to make a difference. And these organizations and programs have grown substantially over time, and in the process, experienced innovations, an increase in talent retention, and have successfully dealt with many challenges. As a business professor, Porter has even founded numerous non-profits, investing his own time and money into varying societal problems. He took the same approach as many before him have taken, but it was that very fact that caused a particularly important realization.

"We've been aware of these problems for decades. We have decades of experience with our NGOs and with our government entities, and there's an awkward reality. The awkward reality is we're not making fast enough progress. We're not winning. These problems still seem very daunting and very intractable, and any solutions we're achieving are small solutions. We're making incremental progress" (Porter).

*   *

Priya Bery recognized this stagnation in the health sector two decades ago, while she was a student at Harvard. I asked her how her career evolved and, what inspired her to be one of the first to create a career that intersected of business and social responsibility?

> When I started this work, I was pursuing a public health degree, and there really wasn't a movement or anything around it. I was a black sheep in that journey, and I was desperately trying to find ways to utilize business to address the public health challenges that we were learning about. And so I was going to the business school, and the public health school, and the urban planning school and trying to create a mini MBA out of all of the different forces, trying to develop a unique way to address these public health issues. And that wasn't a popular thing at that time. And the issue at that time, that was all over the headlines which was the Russia and climate change of today, was 30 million infected with HIV with no access to treatment.

> This was my wake-up moment.

This was a crisis that I grew up with, and it had reached such scale that I was almost paralyzed by it. And so when I learned about different ways to approach it, like MTV at the time, who was finding ways to integrate HIV prevention messages into their story lines…I thought, 'Wow! That's really cool. They know how to change the hearts and minds of young people and they do it all the time. And they can apply that insight and take that influence that they have with that viewer and help them learn something that can save their lives.' And so it led to these ideas that, 'Oh my gosh' moment where I thought, 'That's a big deal.'

And that's where my passion and excitement stemmed from, and that taking a business approach in addressing these issues was not to make money off of it, but to attempt incredible solutions that may not have been realized otherwise because of this different channel of resources and people. And so it was really the first steps of blurring the lines between the public sector, private sector, and the social sector, so that accessing all of that can create all kinds of good. Supporting the idea that it can be very possible and ethical to be making money and do good at the same time. And there are some that do it better than others, and some that are more ethical about it. And when you find a business that does it right at their core, you know that it's real.

*　*

Incremental progress is still progress, but when there are millions of lives depending on this work and our ability to solve problems, incremental progress is not always good enough. And the fundamental problem arising here is that after cutting away all the complexity, it comes down to the fact that we aren't able to scale. We can make progress, we can help hundreds and thousands, sometimes hundreds of thousands, but at the end of the day that's not reaching the goal. Large scale impact still has not been achieved. Why not? (Porter)

Porter points towards a lack of resources. And it's much clearer today than it's been for the past few decades that there is simply not enough money, either in the form of tax revenue or philanthropic donations, to deal with any of the problems that matter at a scale to which they need to be addressed. And this reality needs to be confronted.

So where does business come into play, according to Porter? Well it's actually disproving conventional view that businesses profit more by *causing* social problems, rather than solving them.

> The classic example is pollution. If business pollutes, it makes more money than if it tried to reduce that pollution. Reducing pollution is expensive, therefore businesses

don't want to do it. It's profitable to have an unsafe working environment. It's too expensive to have a safe working environment, therefore business makes more money if they don't have a safe working environment. That's been the conventional wisdom. A lot of companies have fallen into that conventional wisdom. They resisted environmental improvement. They resisted workplace improvement. That thinking has led to, I think, much of the behavior that we have come to criticize in business, that I come to criticize in business. (Porter)

Yet, as Porter began to take on more and more social issues himself, he discovered the opposite was, in fact, true: businesses profited more when they *solved* social issues. The old convention is wrong.

Going back to pollution, it's been found that reducing pollution and emissions is actually generating profit, because it saves money, increases efficiency and productivity, and reduces waste and resource consumption. On top of that, a safe working environment with sound practices and policies in place helps avoid work-related accidents. The exciting thing about this is that we could go issue by issue, finding ways to create economic efficiency without trading social progress. Another example: restaurants. Think of the food waste, everything thrown out at the end of every night!

But this belief that business can achieve this economic efficiency at a profit needs to scale. All business in all industries needs to break out of the conventional wisdom that they don't need to worry about social problems. Instead, they need to change the way they see themselves, and view themselves as actors on a much bigger stage. Porter also agrees that this approach will not be effective without the help of established NGOs creating partnerships with businesses. It's evident that the new NGOs that have created some real change—with the potential to scale—are the ones who have found partnerships and ways to collaborate (Porter).

When businesses see themselves differently, and we change the lens through which society views businesses, the world will change.

*　*

To further build on this idea of changing the way businesses see themselves, the age of judging companies only on heir longevity is passed. The companies that stand the test of the time are the ones that solve problems that matter. It no longer matters how long a company has been on the Fortune 500 list or has maintained a certain leadership. When we really think about the longevity of a business, it's often the bi-product of something more important. Companies that survive "disruptions" and changing markets do so because their mission and purpose stay important.

Google's longevity is a bi-product of the fact that their mission is to organize the world's information. Will all the information in the world ever be completely organized? No, probably not. But every day, it will be one step closer and one step farther, which is why Google will most likely be around for decades to come (Krippendorff).

In the end, companies rarely grow just to grow, or last just to last. Companies scale and thrive when communities, nations, or the world need their mission. Companies committed to solving problems that matter will always be needed, and that's a reason why they will continue to work, grow, and change lives.

What problem keeps your business going?

CHAPTER 7

A NEW STATUS

———

A 2013 survey conducted by Good.Must.Grow., a marketing agency headquartered in Nashville, Tennessee, showed that 63 percent of customers don't always trust corporate claims of social responsibility. This is where "B Corp" status comes in.

B Corps are for-profit companies certified by the nonprofit B Lab to meet rigorous standards of social and environmental performance, accountability, and transparency. Today, there is a growing community of more than 2,100 Certified B Corps from 50 countries, and over 130 industries working together toward one unifying goal: to redefine success in business (B Corporation).

B Corp status is granted according to a rigorous assessment to socially and environmentally conscious companies. To give you an idea of what B Corp status companies look like, here are some of the bigger names: Ben & Jerry's, Patagonia, Etsy, Warby Parker and Cotopaxi, to name a small percentage. These companies are all known for being holistic, mission-driven companies (Bain).

Dermot Hikisch, B Lab's director of business development, adds, "Although many of these are lifestyle brands that have built-in social missions of helping the poor or creating sustainable goods, there are a number of sustainable lawyers, accountants, marketing agencies and financial-service organizations in the mix (Landrum).

To become certified, these businesses must meet a threshold of "impact" compared to their peers, and, in their governing documents, agree that shareholder interests are not the only interests the company will consider. The company also needs to do well by its workers, suppliers, customers, and community. B corporations are different from companies that do good as a sideline; constitutionally, the "do-gooding" is required. If they fail in their social mission, they can be sued, just as traditional shareholder-owned companies can be sued for not pursuing profit aggressively enough (Schiller).

In short, a B Corp certification lets consumers and suppliers know that a particular company is going to pursue, not just profits, but betterment of the world and humanity. It lets consumers know that, rather than just *claiming* certain positive involvements, the company is actually *pursuing* those involvements.

*   *

THE BIG BOYS IN THE MARKET

Today's young people are as concerned with making a positive impact on the world as they are with making money. An astounding 94% want to use their skills to benefit a cause as part of their work. Meanwhile, about half of Americans have confidence in the free market system, down from 80% just 15 years ago. It's obvious that this shift in thinking is more than a trend—it's a full shift. "This is not a fad. It's part of a long-term trend," says Don Shaffer, CEO of RSF Social Finance, an impact-oriented financial services firm in San Francisco. But could major corporations themselves become B corporations?

The first promising signs are popping up with companies like Natura, a large Brazilian cosmetics and toiletries brand, who signed up with B Lab's certification program last year. Unilever, the global manufacturer of multi-category household products (from soap to food) is investigating B-corp status as well. The B-corp movement is a critical part of the shift to a more inclusive and purpose-driven economy, which is unquestionably needed," says Paul Polman, Unilever's CEO.

It would be a very important shift if publicly traded companies like Unilever become B corporations. First off, it would create a new dynamic in how these companies would report their impacts. Rather than just reporting their negative impacts, they could quantify their positive impacts as well. It's a divergence from the trend of just putting out a press release about a new program.

Currently, severarl industries report ESG Metrics which include the fields of environmental, social, and governance. Yet, it is uncertain what is actually done with this information and if it actually meaningful. Most importantly, negative impact disclosure doesn't prevent companies from doing harm, because responsibility rankings routinely recognize companies for depth of disclosure, but pass no judgment on their actual impact. And these disclosures are often without context. "A company will say it saved so much water last year, but it won't tell you about the water conditions where it's operating. The numbers pay no attention to ecological limits, and rely on the market taking care of sustainability problems, even though it doesn't" (Schiller).

"The underlying and unspoken assumption of ESG is that we have a sustainability crisis because we don't have the information. All we need to do is get companies to report and we'll solve the problem. I would argue that markets are just a tool and all the reporting in the world isn't going to solve the problem" says John Fullerton, a former J.P. Morgan managing director and founder of the Capital Institute.

Following in the momentum of B Corps companies like Goldman Sachs, BlackRock, Bain Capital, Zurich, and AXA all now have funds for startups that generate "social returns" alongside profits. There is a lot of capital starting to shift into these areas including hige investments form the likes of Mark Zuckerberg and Priscilla Chan who have pledged to invest most of their $44 billion fortune in impact companies and startups. A survey from J.P. Morgan and the Global Impact Investing Network showed more than $60 billion has already gone into impact investments last year.

This kind of capital definitely helps scale the impact of these organiztions but it also raises the question of whether a company devoted to impact also means its responsible and holds itself to high standards. And so circling back around, that's where B Corp certification completes the holistic approach.

In addition, Leslie Christian, an impact adviser based in Seattle, argues that responsible investing necessarily involves lower returns and a different set of outcomes than, say, putting money into Amazon or GE. "I believe you can make high returns doing impact investing," she says. "You can make a lot of money doing renewable energy, recyclable commodities, or finding a cure to a disease." A Wall Street veteran, Christian says the definition of impact is becoming stretched, with normal sorts of impacts—say, employing people—included. It's no longer about having a responsible impact across stakeholders, just having an impact through the product or service. "[The impact] needs to include all the parties involved, not just the investors, but also customers, suppliers, the natural environment, and the community. That means a fair return to investors, but not an exorbitant return," Christian says. And when you think about it, isn't that what it should be? (Schiller)

*　*

B CORP AS A BUSINESS TOOL

B Lab's self-assessment is an amazing benchmark tool for companies to quickly find ways to mimic socially minded, profitable business models. Greg McEvilly used the B Corp standards as a tool when he launched Rowlett, Texas-based Kammok in 2011, making "zero end waste" outdoor products, such as his signature camping hammock.

"I thought it was a great benchmarking tool," he says of the B Corp survey.

The questionnaire opened his eyes to the benefits of working with local suppliers and distributors. "That was one that I hadn't really thought through," says McEvilly, who got his B Corp status late last year. Although Europe and Asia export the high-quality materials his hammocks call for, he's exploring using fabrics and hardware made closer to home and in developing countries that need jobs. He's also getting ideas that will come in handy when he's ready for a salaried staff, such as flexible work programs for caregivers and time off for employees who volunteer in the community. "Instead of just thinking about profitability, it really expands your horizon," he says (Goodman).

Andrew Stoloff, CEO of Rubicon Bakery, employs 105 full-time staff, some with only a sixth-grade education and many having served time in prison. Stoloff has received plenty of sustainability tips from the B Corp assessment, and he's profited from it. "We're recycling more. We did an energy audit. We retrofitted our lighting. We invested $10,000, and we save $600 a month."

* *

5 REASONS WHY YOU SHOULD BUILD YOUR CORPORATE MISSION MODEL AROUND B CORP STATUS:

1. YOU'LL BUILD A BETTER BUSINESS AND MAKE MORE MONEY

B Corps are many things. They are pro-business, pro-market, pro-environment, pro-good governance and pro-workers.

And interestingly enough, these are not mutually exclusive attributes of a sustainable business. Actually, some of the most well-known organizations, including Accenture, Goldman Sachs, and the *Harvard Business Review*, all concluded that building a sustainable business is overall good for business. On top of that, Raj Sisodia, founder of Conscious Capitalism, found that highly-conscious companies outperformed the S&P 500 by a 14-to-1 ratio over a 15-year period.

Additionally, a recent Nielsen report concluded: "Commitment to social and environmental responsibility is surpassing some of the more traditional influences for many consumers. Brands that fail to take this into account will likely fall behind."

And it cut costs. Being more environmentally and socially conscious reduces energy through initiatives that pay for themselves over time. Creating the inclusive and supportive environment in your tribe reduces employee turnover and saves money on recruitment and training costs.

The B Lab assessment is intended to inspire business owners to think and to nudge them into implementing practices that are good for their businesses. It is, more or less, grading their Corporate Mission Models. And that is a good thing for everyone.

2. YOU'LL JOIN A FAMILY

We have already established that building smart partnerships is advantageous on its own. But forming these as a B Corp brings you into an extensive network of mentors and creative geniuses who are ready to help you along the way. Once you get the B Stamp, you are part of a family that is dedicated to shared interests and a commitment to solving problems that matter (Jacobsen).

3. YOU'LL GET THE X FACTOR OF APPEAL

Millennials, Millennials, Millennials. They're making and breaking businesses today. They're looking for ways to have a social impact with their purchases and the B Stamp is soon to be as enticing as a 50% off tag. A 2014 report from the Boston Consulting Group said that one of the best ways for companies to connect with millennial consumers is by "Convincing millennials that they are 'doing good' when they purchase its brands. In a market where businesses are claiming they do good—but many do not—the B stamp is a proud way to demonstrate your authenticity" (Barton).

4. YOU'LL GET THOSE TALENTED MILLENNIALS...AND KEEP THEM!

B Corps pride themselves on creating a culture around their tribes. These cultures strive to achieve an impact that matters, not just to the CEO or shareholders, but to the employees, as well. This gives your employees purpose and a reason to be excited to come to work every day. Various studies have shown that providing an opportunity to make a difference in the workplace often outranks pay as a motivating factor for young job seekers (Jacobsen).

5. YOU WILL BE DISRUPTIVE

Why not be part of the movement of businesses that have turned conventional business theory on its head? You're a founder, a leader, and a dreamer. You have the mission and your tribe around, you so take the leap. You will look back in the next five to ten years, when B Corp status is the standard for all businesses, and know that you were the disruption that changed the way the world worked (Jacobsen).

CHAPTER 8

CROWD INVESTING

—

CROWD-FUNDING IS CHANGING EVERYTHING

Startups don't have to convince Venture Capitalists and Impact Investors in person, anymore. Today, startups can lift their businesses off the ground quickly, backed by crowd-funding—literally, by people who believe what they believe. Starting with Kickstarter and then raising equity capital through organizations like FundersClub, these startup companies have the possibility of rapidly becoming Series A businesses. Quick definition: A Series A round is the name typically given to a company's first significant round of venture capital financing. The name refers to the class of preferred stock sold to investors in exchange for their investment (Narasin).

In a world with choices though, finding the right fundraising strategy can be very hard, especially when you have multiple target audiences. At the same time, the rewards of putting in the time to raise capital the right way are huge. Crowd-Funding has led to the ability of startup businesses to build and grow a dedicated and enthusiastic fan and customer base, find backing for ideas and missions that would have been passed over otherwise, and has created the potential to create a movement.

Talking with Ari Krasner, the conversation turned to his initial development of GiveButter's platform, and, with that, came the inevitable topic of raising capital.

> ME: What were the goals of GiveButter?
> ARI: It seems like there is a problem with the fundraising industry. Many of the fundraising platforms are not accomplishing what they want to accomplish. And we couldn't really fill that gap. And that's kind of what initially started us on the Give Butter path—creating a crowd-attracting platform.

And the idea is the same here with two goals here, right? One is build an amazing company and to really be able to make some really positive changes in the industry and change the way fundraising is done online. Build an amazing company, a big company, that's gonna make a global impact very soon.

The second is it's not just the business and money and success, it's also just how we can make the largest impact in the world with this company that we're building. And we're in a unique position to do that because we're college students. We believe in what we're doing, and it's working. So how can we build an incredibly successful company, one that people love, one that helps change this industry, and one that helps people do really amazing things?

How do we take what we've done and really benefit the world? It would be almost selfish for us to not actually care about that. And there're separate things we're working on for the future, incredibly powerful things that will be a huge impact. So it's just as much about social good, particularly in the long run.

*   *

Crowd-funding has enabled, really, the entire world to give to something in which they are interested; everyone can become a small-time investor in something that matters to them. It's created an environment where social entrepreneurs and new businesses can learn rapidly, build support programs, raise growth capital, engage philanthropists and investors, and build a movement.

Historically, entrepreneurs needed to pitch a spectacular, fully-developed business plan to traditional investors. But what this created was a tunnel vision of approach: entrepreneurs had to tailor their business to the likes of the investor, and not the consumer. Crowdfunding solves this conventional problem.

It allows entrepreneurs to consider more than just their shareholders, but also their partnerships, clients, and consumers. The platforms are committed to innovative technology, to causes, and creativity-fueled campaigns. Slave Rubin, the co-founder and CEO of the crowdfunding platform, Indiegogo, explains that with more than 100,000 campaigns under its belt, nine million unique monthly visitors and more than $16 million in funding, the company has certainly lived up to its motto: "We empower people to fund what matters."

In addition to helping a business get off the ground, crowdfunding is an efficient way to fill the gap between initial investment and the funding needed for startups to "go to market." This is usually a time when resources are tight, and it is a crucial time in a business's first opportunity to scale. Crowdfunding can provide the quick funds and resources that businesses need to expand and grow after getting their feet off the ground.

Take Maria Springer and LivleyHoods, her youth economic opportunities program in Kenya. She had gotten the funding for her first location and had huge success with it. She wanted to expand and scale to the next level, so she raised $25,000 on Indiegogo under the theme of doing more than just providing a bandage to cover up poverty, but being a real part of the solution. She went a step farther and put 25 adhesive bandages on her face and peeled each one off every time she raised $1,000 dollars. It only took 25 days to peel off the last one, with a final funding of $27,074 from 251 people. Her second store is up and running, and the scaling continues.

Crowdfunding is valuable, not only for supporting the expansion of a business, but also the expansion of an idea. It is a unique approach to opening our minds to new perspectives in the world.

Simon Griffiths used crowdfunding, along with his toilet paper distribution company, Who Gives a Crap, to advocate for the global sanitation crisis that our society faces. More than 2.4 billion people do not have access to toilets, something that many of us take for granted in our everyday lives. Simon's toilet paper line contributes half of their profits to sanitation initiatives throughout the developing world.

To begin to scale, Simon needed to raise at least $50,000. He took a unique approach to making his efforts known: live-streaming himself sitting on a toilet seat until he raised his goal. Simon created a sense of urgency and demonstrated his purpose quite clearly. It worked. His campaign produced an amazing response, raising more than $65,000 and, at the same time, changing the perspective of 9000+ campaign viewers worldwide.

The value of crowdfunding is not limited solely to raising capital. Investors are also using crowdfunding efforts as a way to predict success based off the demand for their product or service and it is evident that crowdfunding has become a valuable tool in the social entrepreneur's toolbox. It is inspiring to see crowdfunding support an era of togetherness in social innovation, especially in an era often celebrated for its individualism. Ari's initiative with GiveButter encapsulates the goal of bringing millions together.

ME: What's the story behind GiveButter?

ARI: About a year and a half ago, Snowstorm Joan attacked, and we essentially locked ourselves in a room for 4 days, because we knew that we were gonna have Monday off and we knew who's gonna be snowed out, and so we almost did not leave the room for four days. We brought in food and we had everything we needed, so we didn't have to leave. And I think I left once, for four days... And what we did is we decided that we wanted to build something fast, we wanted to build something big, and somebody would receive the impact of it after just four days.

And so what we did is we built, at the time, was called The Big Catch Game. Essentially what it was…is {a} website that was based on the 2005 million dollar home-page concept, where we sold ads based on website and we essentially sold people on the fact they could buy ads based website. But we wanted to be different, we want to give money back to people instead on taking it for ourselves so we created to that all you need is to do is enter your email for a chance to win the money that is in the pot from below these ads. We have around 430,000 entries over $2200.

We finished it but the thing is the I came into the room when my roommates were talking and I said, 'Guys, I think we should add a giving back component. I think we should make it a charitable thing so that our impact, you know, goes beyond the one weekend, and if this turns into something significant, we can make some really cool change in the world. We can do really well by ourselves and do really good.' So why wouldn't we do both when we were perfectly capable of incorporating a social aspect? That was very easy to do.

So as soon as we had this idea, my two roommates at the time loved that. So at the time we took before the 4 weeks was just right during the weekend changed a couple days later, we changed from the Big Catch Game to the concept was we give the cash to you if you win, but also to the charity of your choice. And the whole concept was the winner of the Sweepstakes at the end 4 weeks had to give 18% of the winnings to charity. It's an organization of their choice. And additionally we work hard to sort different partnerships with really large profits that we could feature them website the home page.

The idea is like thousands of college students coming in and young people and people all over are checking the website all over the world and entering this crazy sweepstakes and we wanted to not only make the winner give back we were also offering space to non-profits and we were featuring these really great organizations. All over the world like Red Cross, the World Wildlife Fund. And essentially what inspired me to bring this up in the first place is that I felt this was an injustice to aim to build something that would ultimately provide us a lot of benefits where we easily could benefit others and the rest of the world in really positive way and a powerful one. It was like let's take this social good and make it big with us like we'll be doing 2 things at the same time and it made just a ton of logical steps. You know we wanted this Sweepstakes to have to be the biggest thing in the world, and we wanted everyone and their mother to apply. But we also thought this could be a really great platform also just to make sure that if it does spiral, out of control in a good way. And if there is millions of dollars in the winning pot it could be an amazing opportunity for people to give back and we would have inspired that. And from this idea GiveButter was born.

*   *

HERE'S WHAT YOU NEED TO DO TO BE A SUCCESSFUL CROWD-FUNDER:

UNDERSTAND WHO YOU ARE WORKING WITH BEFORE YOU START

You don't want to go into anything blind as a founder or leader of your company, so do your homework both on and offline before choosing a platform through which to fundraise. Talk to other successful campaigns that have used the same platform and understand what the process looks like and how it will add value to your mission.

BE PREPARED

Get your company to a place where it is poised to share its purpose with the world. You need people to believe in you as much as you believe in yourself. If you've had meaningful interactions with potential consumers or investors, make those known.

BE CRYSTAL CLEAR AND HIT THE KEY POINTS

Be completely transparent and authentic about exactly what your product or service does, how it works, and how it serves as part of your mission. There's nothing more powerful to a potential investor than a clear message and vision that their money will help create. Avoid the buzzwords, and, instead, communicate *value.*

In addition, get feedback from people you trust—fellow founders, advisors, other investors—and see what questions come up the most often about your startup. Those will likely be the questions that other potential investors will have, and you want to have good, well thought-out answers ahead of time. You may only have one shot to clearly communicate your message.

"The information you post should be no different than what an offline investor would look for. Hit the main points: What is the idea? How does the product or service work? Who's on the team? What key milestones have you hit? What are your metrics for success? What is the market size potential? What are the investment terms? How big is the round you're trying to raise? Ideally, you have a pitch deck that works without you being there to explain it."

ME: Can you give me one piece of advice that you would give if I were embarking on my own startup tomorrow with GiveButter?

ARI: Make sure that you believe in what you're doing, know what's going on with how you treat our customers, and how you treat everyone on your platform to create an impact that you can scale with your success.

CHAPTER 9

THE NEW DO-GOODERS

——

No matter what anybody tells you, words and ideas can change the world. And the human race is filled with passion. And medicine, law, business, engineering—these are noble pursuits and necessary to sustain life. But poetry, beauty, romance, love— these are what we stay alive for. That you are here; that life exists; and identity. That the powerful play goes on, and you may contribute a verse. What will your verse be?

—ROBIN WILLIAMS

I came across this quote one night while scrolling through my social media page. It was a video, really, with the uplifting music building behind it, and I watched one of my favorite childhood actors inspire a group of students to pursue meaning in life above all else. It was really powerful in that moment and I desperately wanted to experience all the things that we are "alive" for.

I started thinking about how today, this rejuvenation of purpose and mission is built into companies, and how this mixing is bringing Williams' inspiring and uplifting theory of life into all different industries. Careers and businesses are no longer *just* a means to make money and sustain a comfortable life; they are becoming more beautiful in themselves, giving people the opportunity to contribute each of their unique verses to what is, ultimately, the Song of Humanity.

Here are some of the passionate do-gooders and their businesses—their songs—that I've come to admire.

DO-GOODER: LEILA JANAH

FOUNDER AND CEO OF SAMASOURCE AND LXMI,
AND AN AWARD WINNING SOCIAL ENTREPRENEUR

CORPORATE MISSION MODEL

"Leila Janah is on a mission to eradicate poverty. She dismantles the current thinking on charity and the West's view of those most in need; she shows how traditional aid is broken, and argues that the solution rests in progressive business models, weaving together private, public, and nonprofit sectors" (Acast).

Janah did not go the typical route applying for grants to start her company. Rather, she uses the extensive network she built to raise $2 million, funding and launching Laxmi.

"LXMI's primary ingredient harvests enables its producers to earn at least 3x local wages" (LXMI).

Janah made conscious efforts developing LXMI to build non-profit collectives right into her supply chain. She and her team believe that work creates pride, fair pay creates satisfaction, and pride and satisfaction create a product worth selling.

However, paying more than triple the average regional wage does more than produce a nice skin cream, it helps alleviate some of the more serious issues facing the world—at least in the regions where her skincare ingredients are grown. Because the workers are well-paid, their areas are seeing declines in serious problems, such as malnutrition, starvation and human trafficking (LXMI).

NUGGETS OF KNOWLEDGE

I was shocked at how easy it was to raise money as a for-profit business. This is where building that network is huge! It's 2017,

DO-GOODER: ELEANOR ALLEN

WATER FOR PEOPLE

CORPORATE MISSION MODEL

Everyone needs access to clean and drinkable water. That's sort of a given. But around the world, nearly two billion people don't have access to it. That's almost 25% of the world's population. Water for People, and its founder, Eleanor Allen, believes this is unacceptable.

Allen, whose background includes civil engineering and serving in the Peace Corp, founded Water for People in 1991. Her organization works closely with world governments to improve and, in some cases, provide water sanitation services. At the rate they are growing, they will reach 40 million people within half a decade (WaterForPeople.com).

Water changes everything. It lays the foundation for health, education and economic prosperity. That is social progress.

—ELEANOR ALLEN

DO-GOODERS: ZACHARY QUINN AND BRIAN KELLER

CO-FOUNDERS OF LOVE YOUR MELON

CORPORATE MISSION MODEL

Love Your Melon began selling winter beanies in 2012 on a "buy one, give one" model—for every hat sold, Love Your Melon donated a hat to a child with cancer. Their model was so successful that they soon changed their model to include investing 50% of their profits to fund cancer research initiatives and provide immediate support for families of children battling cancer. They also reinvested some of those prophets to diversifying their product from just beanies to include t-shirts, headbands and other accessories. They also have plans to further expand, becoming a full apparel line (MacBride).

Zachary Quinn and Brian Keller, who founded the company when they were both still in college, have used that to their advantage: they have "set up shop," so to speak, in more than eight hundred college campuses across the United States, employing more than 13,000 college students. These students do more than just sell hats, though: they spend a good deal of their time educating people about the realities of childhood cancer, and discussing the ways in which *their* company—because all of them are invested in it—helps families who have been hit hard with these realties. Started by millennials and focusing on reach millennials, Love Your Melon is a living example of what a social-conscious business can accomplish (Palasz).

NUGGETS OF KNOWLEDGE

Of course, companies with the best branding have always created communities—but listening to Quinn talk about Love Your Melon's identity and its use of Facebook made me realize how much easier and faster doing so is with social media. Love Your Melon—a consumer product company—was able to scale nationally in less than five years.

—FORBES MAGAZINE

DO-GOODER: JEREMY JOHNSON

CO-FOUNDER AND CEO OF ANDELA

CORPORATE MISSION MODEL

Similar to Leilah Janah's philosophy of "Give Work," Jeremy Johnson founded Andela with the goal of seeking out and training Africa's top developers, and then "integrat{ing} them into the world's best tech companies" (Andela.com). One of the companies that Johnson works with is Payoff, a financial service company that helps its clients get out of credit card debt. Talk about making a difference on more than one level.

NUGGETS OF KNOWLEDGE

When a business is in its early stages, everything keeps you awake. I worry about helping to create structure to support scale and making sure we are finding the best possible placements in companies for the fellows in the programme. I worry about how we are training them, not just to be world class software developers but world class human beings and leaders. We are doing a pretty good job, obviously, but one can always do better. One of the hallmarks of Andela and our culture is the recognition that you can always do better. Andelans are constantly seeking to improve and learn.

—JEREMY JOHNSON

DO-GOODER—DAVIS SMITH

FOUNDER AND CEO OF COTOPAXI, CERTIFIED B CORP

CORPORATE MISSION MODEL

Davis Smith founded his company, Cotopaxi, on two premises:

- Provide high-quality outdoor gear
- Change the world

It's the last point that really drives Smith in everything he does. As one of the first businesses to become certified as a Benefit Corporation, Cotopaxi uses—at minimum—ten percent of their profits to impact people all over the globe. As a few examples, your purchases from Cotopaxi can help provide six months of clean water to a person in India, or provide a weeks' worth of education for a Peruvian child (Sarumi).

NUGGETS OF KNOWLEDGE

Sometimes we feel like the world is such a scary place and it's just getting worse, and certainly there are things to be concerned about, but when we look at the world as a whole, the world is becoming much better," Smith said. *"I believe we can eradicate extreme poverty in our lifetimes but can't depend on the government alone to do that or nonprofits by themselves. We need the private sector to play their part. There are a lot of really beautiful, promising things about what's happening in the world right now, and we can be a part of that (Jones).*

The 1980s model of corporate social responsibility was to throw some money at something at the end of the year," Smith says. " Today for most businesses their largest market is Millennials who value experiences more than things. Your product has to tell a story that resonates. You can't just compete on the best technical performance, or make the best backpack anymore. You have to go deeper, and make a human connection that's meaningful (Lane Taylor).

—DAVIS SMITH

DO-GOODERS—DAVID FOSTER AND SAM POLK

CO-FOUNDERS OF EVERYTABLE

CORPORATE MISSION MODEL

Everytable has one mission: good food on every table. Foster and Polk, founders of Everytable, aim to renovate and revolutionize the fast-food industry by providing healthier, more nutritionally-balanced food, but at the speed and—close to—cost of the major fast-food chains (Everytable).

Prior to opening their stores in mid-2016, "health food" restaurants were located solely in affluent areas, and were massively overpriced, to say the least. Foster and Polk made it their mission to bring the same quality food to poorer areas of Los Angeles—where they are based—but at fast-food prices, and thus was the birth of Everytable. But they didn't stop there.

They also opened locations in the wealthier areas of Los Angeles, but at slightly less of the cost of most of the other "health food" stores. But why charge wealthier people more for the same food?

Because, like it or not, healthier food *is* more expensive to produce, ship, and store, and by creating a higher profit margin in some areas, Everytable can afford to provide the same food with little to no profit in poorer areas. Good food on every table (Enso).

NUGGETS OF KNOWLEDGE

And most importantly: we wanted a brand that could serve as a beacon not just for a company, but for a shared mission. Something that people could not just buy from, but join, for the good of themselves, their family and community (Enso).

—DAVID FOSTER AND SAM POLK

DO-GOODER:EILEEN FISHER

FOUNDER AND PRESIDENT OF EILEEN FISHER
CLOTHING LINE, CERTIFIED B CORP

CORPORATE MISSION MODEL

Fisher's vision goes beyond fashion, because she believes that a well-run business should be able to afford leaving the world a better place. She invests the company's profits into her supply chain, which she has expanded to near-global capacity, helping poverty-level workers find good work and decent pay. She reinvests the company's money into finding better, more sustainable methods of production, non-toxic dyes for her clothing lines, and is committed to reducing carbon output and use (Fisher).

According to *Fortune*, the company is now worth more than $400 million. It sounds like it's working.

NUGGETS OF KNOWLEDGE

About three years ago, when Eileen Fisher began focusing specifically on reducing its impact, it started from a core group of a dozen or so decision makers across different parts of the company. Slowly but steadily it has brought more people into the discussion, through in-person workshops and a presentation

DO-GOODER—ADAM LOWRY AND ERIC RYAN

METHOD, CERTIFIED B CORP

CORPORATE MISSION MODEL

Eleven years after it launched, Method did something innovative: they began packaging their soaps in plastics made, largely, from ocean trash. Considering they manufacture their soaps using completely natural components taken from sustainable sources, and Method has managed to tackle two problems for the price of one (Method).

And it shows.

In 2012, they posted $100 million revenues. They also merged with Ecover (a Belgian B Corp), becoming the largest green company in the world. Together, they bring in over $300 million in revenue, a percentage of which is reinvested in their local communities, as well as their drive to be completely sustainable (Method).

Kick Ass at Fast: Use small size to your advantage; by bringing innovations to market faster, you can stay out in front of larger rivals (Lowry, Ryan).

—ADAM LOWRY AND ERIC RYAN

CHAPTER 10

CLOSING THOUGHTS

———

Laurence D. Fink, CEO of the global investment firm, is a millennial. Not in age, mind you, but certainly in thought and action. His firm holds and handles more than $6 trillion in assets, but he has made it clear that if you want him to invest in your business, your business needs to be investing in the community and world.

This is the momentum of a movement, and it is definitely momentum when the world's largest investor says aloud and declares that he plans to hold companies accountable. It is the scaling of the evolution of corporate America, and soon the global corporate world. BlackRock is adding staff to monitor how companies respond to this call to action.

Fink also points out that he is seeing, "many governments failing to prepare for the future, on issues ranging from retirement and infrastructure to automation and worker retraining.," He then adds, "As a result, society increasingly is turning to the private sector and asking that companies respond to broader societal challenges."

And while Fink emphasizes social contributions from companies, he also stresses the importance of profits, and the continued conversation as social purpose is increasingly linked to a company's ability to maintain its profits.

Fink has adopted the millennial mindset, realizing the direction that business and society have chosen moving forward. And while it seems out of the ordinary for one of the largest investors on Wall Street to make this declaration, it has poised itself to become the norm in the coming years (Sorkin).

This is the mindset that has created the Corporate Mission Model. It has intertwined business, profit, and purpose into a growing force, tumbling forward at an increasing speed. It is propelled by optimism and thrives on authenticity. Priya Bery prioritizes authenticity above all else, because even if you're the best and most charitable company in the world, if it's a horrible place to work, people will know that. And so it's connecting all aspects throughout your model.

Business is evolving. It is starting to see itself as a system that can solve problems that matter, just as we are starting to see our identity mirrored by our investments. When we change the lens through which society and businesses view themselves, the world will change.

ACKNOWLEDGMENTS

This book would not have been possible without the "giving" spirit of so many people. I would like to thank Eric, Anastasia, Brian and the rest of the Creator Institute Team for the many hours devoted to me and my experience. And to the many people that read my drafts and helped turn my research and ideas into something decently interesting to read. Lastly, thank you to my parents for supporting me in all my passions. I would never had thought I'd be able to call myself an author. Yet, as Eric said before, "This is only your first book." And now, I actually believe him.

BIBLIOGRAPHY

INTRODUCTION

Shawbel, Dan. "Neil Blumenthal: What Hes Learned From The
Success Of Warby Parker." *Forbes*, Forbes Magazine, 23 Dec.
2016, Web. www.forbes.com/sites/danschawbel/2016/12/23/
neil-blumenthal-what-hes-learned-from-the-success-of-war-
by-parker/#3d3d2c567143.

Parker, Warby. "Warby Parker." Warby Parker, Warby Parker, 22
Nov. 2017. Warby Parker Official Website, Web. https://www.
warbyparker.com/

Andersen, Erika. "Why You're Having A Hard Time With
Your Millennial Employees—And What To Do About
It." *Forbes*, Forbes Magazine, 29 June 2016, Web.
www.forbes.com/sites/erikaandersen/2016/05/09/

why-youre-having-a-hard-time-with-your-millenial-employ-
ees-and-what-to-do-about-it/#33985bae41c5

CHAPTER ONE

Brucella, Giana. "Givebutter Builds a Better
Way to Fundraise." *Nobly*, Nobly.com, Feb.
2017, Web. www.nobly.com/2017/02/06/
givebutter-builds-a-better-way-to-fundraise/.

Lapidos, Juliet. "Wait, What, I'm a Millennial?" *The New York
Times*, The New York Times, 4 Feb. 2015, Web. www.nytimes.
com/2015/02/05/opinion/wait-what-im-a-millennial.html.

Walkom, Renee. "Millennials—The Viewpoint of an Insider."
LinkedIn, 12 Dec. 2017, Web. www.linkedin.com/pulse/
millennials-viewpoint-insider-ren%C3%A9e-walkom-mba/.

Deloitte. "The Millennial Majority Is Transforming Your Culture
| Deloitte US." *Deloitte United States*, Deloitte, 3 July 2017,
Web. www2.deloitte.com/us/en/pages/about-deloitte/arti-
cles/millennial-majority-transforming-culture.html. This
report was developed in collaboration with the Billie Jean
King Leadership Initiative (BJKLI), a nonprofit organization founded by Billie Jean King in partnership with Teneo
as part of an effort to encourage companies, corporations,
and individuals to embrace those with diverse personali-
ties, backgrounds, and lifestyles for the positive and unique
contributions they bring to the workforce

Jarrett, Christian. "We Have an Ingrained Anti-Profit Bias That

Blinds Us to the Social Benefits of Free Markets." *Research Digest*, BPS Research Digest, 7 Aug. 2017, Web. digest.bps.org. uk/2017/08/04/we-have-an-ingrained-anti-profit-bias-that-blinds-us-to-the-social-benefits-of-free-markets/

Fromm, Jeff. "Millennials In The Workplace: They Don't Need Trophies But They Want Reinforcement." *Forbes*, Forbes Magazine, 15 Mar. 2016, Web. www.forbes.com/sites/jefffromm/2015/11/06/ millennials-in-the-workplace-they-dont-need-trophies-but-they-want-reinforcement/#1b08a01453f6.

Singal, Jesse. "Are You an Old Millennial or a Young Millennial?" CNN, Cable News Network, 1 May 2017, Web. www.cnn. com/2017/05/01/health/young-old-millennial-partner/index. html.

OfficeVibe. "20 Statistics About Millennials in the Workplace." *SlideShare*, LinkedIn, 4 Aug. 2016, Web. www.slideshare.net/ Officevibe/20-statistics-about-millennials-in-the-workplace.

CHAPTER TWO

Rosamaria C. Moura-Leite, Robert C. Padgett, (2011) "Historical background of corporate social responsibility", Social Responsibility Journal, Vol. 7 Issue: 4, pp.528-539, https://doi. org/10.1108/17471111111117511

Landrum, Sarah. "Millennials Driving Brands To Practice Socially Responsible Marketing." *Forbes*, Forbes Magazine, 17 Mar. 2017, Web. www.

forbes.com/sites/sarahlandrum/2017/03/17/
millennials-driving-brands-to-practice-socially-responsi-
ble-marketing/#6173c10e4990.

McClimon, Timothy J. "The Shape of Corporate Philanthropy
Yesterday and Today."*Grantmakers in the Arts*, Council on
Foundations, 2003, Web. www.giarts.org/article/shape-cor-
porate-philanthropy-yesterday-and-today. Timothy J.
McClimon is executive director, Second Stage Theatre.
Before going to Second Stage, he was executive director,
AT&T Foundation, and for six years he served on the board
of GIA.

CHAPTER THREE

Bellis, Rich. "Here's What Millennials Want From Their
Performance Reviews." *Fast Company*, Fast Company, 6 Nov.
2015, Web. www.fastcompany.com/3052988/heres-what-mil-
lennials-want-from-their-performance-reviews.

Oppong, Thomas. "Don't Just Start a Business, Solve a Problem."
The Globe and Mail, 2014 Entrepreneur Media, Inc, 25

Enso. "Launching a Shared Mission: Good Food on Every Table."
Medium, Enso Ideas, 28 July 2016, Web. medium.com/enso/
launching-a-shared-mission-good-food-on-every-table-
76cfbcc334e4

Lane Taylor, Peter. "Gear For Good: Outdoor Start-Up
Cotopaxi On Why Millennials Want Stories, Not
Things." *Forbes Startup Life*, Forbes, 30 Jan. 2017,
Web. www.forbes.com/sites/petertaylor/2017/01/30/

gear-for-good-outdoor-start-up-cotopaxi-on-why-millenni-
als-want-stories-not-things/4/#29b4599a2244

MacBride, Elizabeth. "How A Minnesota Startup Scaled To
$40 Million Selling U.S.-Manufactured Clothes." *Forbes*,
Forbes Magazine, 5 July 2017, Web. www.forbes.com/sites/
elizabethmacbride/2017/06/30/love-your-melons-founder-
on-how-to-scale-nationally-using-facebook/3/#47332e456740

Mahmud, Adeeb. "Beyond Charity: Three Innovative Types of
Business Partnerships for Nonprofits." *Guardian Sustainable
Business*, The Gaurdian, Feb. 2014, Web. www.theguardian.
com/sustainable-business/ngo-business-nonprofit-partner-
ships-gsk-nespresso-wwf-coke.

Schiller, Ben. "Never Mind Corporate Responsibility, Companies
Can Solve Actual Social Problems." *Fast Company*,
Fast Company, 9 Jan. 2015, Web. www.fastcompany.
com/3039695/never-mind-corporate-responsibility-compa-
nies-can-solve-actual-social-problems.

Sivers, Derek. "Tribes—by Seth Godin." *Tribes*, Web. sivers.org/
book/Tribes.

Yu, Emily. "How Millennials Are Driving the Future of Social
Entrepreneurship." *The Case Foundation*, The Case
Foundation, Aug. 2015, Web. casefoundation.org/blog/
how-millennials-are-driving-future-social-entrepreneurship/

CHAPTER FOUR

B Lab. "GIIRS Funds." B Analytics, B Lab, Web. b-analytics.net/
giirs-funds (http://b-analytics.net/giirs-funds).

Mahmud, Adeeb. "Beyond Charity: Three Innovative Types of
Business Partnerships for Nonprofits." Guardian Sustainable
Business, The Guardian, Feb. 2014, Web. www.theguardian.
com/sustainable-business/ngo-business-nonprofit-partner-
ships-gsk-nespresso-wwf-coke (http://www.theguardian.
com/sustainable-business/ngo-business-nonprofit-partner-
ships-gsk-nespresso-wwf-coke).

"Prime Minister: 'Social Investment Can Be a Great Force for
Social Change.'" Gov.UK Speech, Crown Copyright, 5 July
2AD, Web. www.gov.uk/government/speeches/prime-minis-
ters-speech-at-the-social-impact-investment-conference.

Sir Ronald Cohen and William A. Sahlman. "Social Impact
Investing Will Be the New Venture Capital." Harvard
Business Review, Harvard Business Review, 30 Nov. 2017,
Web. hbr.org/2013/01/social-impact-investing-will-b (http://
hbr.org/2013/01/social-impact-investing-will-b).

CHAPTER FIVE

Ballif, Natasha. "National Parks Traveler." *National
Parks*, National Parks Traveler, Dec. 2014,
Web. www.nationalparkstraveler.org/2014/12/
cotopaxi-gear-manufacturer-paying-it-forward25959.

Jones, Morgan. " Do Good: Cotopaxi Founder and CEO Seeks
to Change the World, Starting in Salt Lake City." *Desert
News*, Desert News, Dec. 2016, Web. www.deseretnews.com/
article/865669281/Do-good-Cotopaxi-founder-and-CEO-
seeks-to-change-the-world-starting-in-Salt-Lake-City.html.

Montague, Ty. "The Rise Of Storydoing: Inside The Staggering
Success Of Toms Shoes." *Fast Company*, Fast Company, 6
Aug. 2013, Web. www.fastcompany.com/3015209/the-rise-of-
storydoing-inside-the-staggering-success-of-toms-shoes.

Sarumi, Ahrif. "Outdoor Company Cotopaxi Puts Its Money
Where Its Heart Is." *The Huffington Post*, TheHuffingtonPost.
com, 28 Aug. 2014, Web. www.huffingtonpost.com/ahrif-sa-
rumi/cotopaxi-put-its-money-where-its-heart-is_b_5710167.
html.

Smith, Davis, and Asialene Smith. "Cotopaxi." *Cotopaxi, Gear
For Good*, Facebook, Oct. 2017, Web. www.facebook.com/
cotopaxigear/videos/1698412640234033/.

Widrich, Leo. "The Science of Storytelling: Why Telling a Story Is
the Most Powerful Way to Activate Our Brains." *Lifehacker*,
Lifehacker.com, 5 Dec. 2012, Web. lifehacker.com/5965703/
the-science-of-st

CHAPTER SIX

Bornstein, David. "The Rise of the Social Entrepreneur."
The New York Times, The New York Times, 13 Nov.
2012, Web. opinionator.blogs.nytimes.com/2012/11/13/
the-rise-of-social-entrepreneur/

Harrison, Scott. "Scott's Story." *We Believe We Can End The Water
Crisis In Our Lifetime*, Charity Water, 2006, Web. www.char-
itywater.org/about/scott-harrison-story/

Krippendorff, Kaihan. "Great Companies Solve Problems
That Matter." *Fast Company*, Fast Company, 17

Dec. 2013, Web. www.fastcompany.com/3023216/
great-companies-solve-problems-that-matter

Porter, Michael. "The Case for Letting Business Solve Social
Problems." *TED: Ideas Worth Spreading*, TED.com, 2013,
Web. www.ted.com/talks/michael_porter_why_busi-
ness_can_be_good_at_solving_social_problems/
transcript

CHAPTER SEVEN

Bain, Mick. "Should Your Startup Take the Public Benefit
or B Corp Route?" *TechCrunch*, TechCrunch, 2
Oct. 2016, Web. techcrunch.com/2016/10/02/
should-your-startup-take-the-b-corp-route/.

Barton, Christine, et al. " How Millennials Are Changing
the Face of Marketing Forever." *The Reciprocity Principle*,
Boston Consulting Group, Jan. 2014, Web. www.bcg.com/
publications/2014/marketing-center-consumer-customer-in-
sight-how-millennials-changing-marketing-forever.aspx.

B Corporation. "B Corporation." *What Are B Corps? | B
Corporation*, BCorporation.net, Web. www.bcorporation.net/
what-are-b-corps.

Change, B the. "So, You Want to Start Your Business as a
Benefit Corp, But Don't Know Where to Start." *B The
Change*, B The Change, 22 Aug. 2017, Web. bthechange.com/
so-you-want-to-start-your-business-as-a-benefit-corp-but-
dont-know-where-to-start-ba87d57ea0c7.

Fox, MeiMei. "5 Reasons Why Social Entrepreneurship
Is The New Business Model." *Forbes*, Forbes
Magazine, 8 Aug. 2016, Web. www.forbes.com/sites/
meimeifox/2016/08/08/5-reasons-why-social-entrepreneur-
ship-is-the-new-business-model/#ee0600b44ca7.

Goodman, Michelle. "Everything You Need to Know About
B Corporation Certification."*Entrepreneur*, Entrepreneur
Magazine, 6 Aug. 2013, Web. www.entrepreneur.com/
article/227099.

Jacobsen, Scott. "6 Reasons Why Every Startup Should
Become a B Corporation." *Done Good*, DoneGood.
com, June 2009, Web. blog.donegood.co/2016/06/29/
startup-become-b-corporation/

Landrum, Sarah. "Millennials Driving Brands To
Practice Socially Responsible Marketing."*Forbes*,
Forbes Magazine, 17 Mar. 2017, Web. www.
forbes.com/sites/sarahlandrum/2017/03/17/
millennials-driving-brands-to-practice-socially-responsi-
ble-marketing/#6173c10e4990.

Schiller, Ben. "Never Mind Corporate Responsibility, Companies
Can Solve Actual Social Problems." *Fast Company*,
Fast Company, 9 Jan. 2015, Web. www.fastcompany.
com/3039695/never-mind-corporate-responsibility-compa-
nies-can-solve-actual-social-problems.

CHAPTER EIGHT

Narasin, Ben. "Series A Round." *Wikipedia*, Wikimedia Foundation, 28 Feb. 2018, Web. en.wikipedia.org/wiki/Series_A_round.

Round, First. "How Crowd-Funding Is Changing Everything and What That Means for Your Startup." *First Round Review*, FirstRound.com, 29 Jan. 2015, Web. firstround.com/review/How-Crowd-Funding-Is-Changing-Everything-and-What-That-Means-for-Your-Startup/.

Zipkin, Nina. "If I Knew Then: Indiegogo Co-Founder Makes His Mark Helping Others Follow Their Passion." *Entrepreneur*, Entrepreneur Magazine, 9 Jan. 2014, Web. www.entrepreneur.com/article/230714.

CHAPTER NINE

Acast. "296: How Leila Janah Is Embarking on Her Mission To Eradicate Poverty By Giving Work | As Told By Nomads on Acast." *Acast*, 6 Oct. 2017, Web. www.acast.com/astoldbynomads/296-howleilajanahisembarkingonhermissiontoeradicatepovertybygivingwork.

Allen, Eleanor. "Water For People." *About Eleanor*, Water For People, Web. www.waterforpeople.org/about/eleanor/.

Andela. "This Is Andela—Meet the Team." *Andela*, Andela.com, Web. andela.com/about-us/.

Bain, Marc. "For Eileen Fisher, a Leader in Sustainable Fashion, Perfection Isn't the Point." *Quartz*, Quartz Media LLC, 22 Apr.

2106, Web. qz.com/661315/for-eileen-fisher-a-leader-in-sus-
tainable-fashion-perfection-isnt-the-point/.

Enso. "Launching a Shared Mission: Good Food on Every Table."
Medium, Enso Ideas, 28 July 2016, medium.com/enso/
launching-a-shared-mission-good-food-on-every-table-
76cfbcc334e4

Everytable. "Mission." *Everytable*, Everytable.com, Web. www.
everytable.com/mission.

Fisher, Eileen. "Vision 2020." *Vision 2020 | Eileen Fisher*,
EileenFisher.com, Web. www.eileenfisher.com/vision-2020/.

Janah, Leila. "Leila Janah." *Leila Janah*, LeilaJanah.com, 2016,
Web. www.leilajanah.com/.

Jones, Morgan. " Do Good: Cotopaxi Founder and CEO Seeks
to Change the World, Starting in Salt Lake City." *Desert
News*, Desert News, Dec. 2016, Web. www.deseretnews.com/
article/865669281/Do-good-Cotopaxi-founder-and-CEO-
seeks-to-change-the-world-starting-in-Salt-Lake-City.html.

Lane Taylor, Peter. "Gear For Good: Outdoor Start-Up
Cotopaxi On Why Millennials Want Stories, Not
Things." *Forbes Startup Life*, Forbes, 30 Jan. 2017,
Web. www.forbes.com/sites/petertaylor/2017/01/30/
gear-for-good-outdoor-start-up-cotopaxi-on-why-millenni-
als-want-stories-not-things/4/#29b4599a2244

Lowry, Adam, and Eric Ryan. *The Method Method: Seven
Obsessions That Helped Our Scrappy Start-up Turn an
Industry Upside Down*. Portfolio, 2011.

LXMI. "Organic & Natural Skincare Brand | Luxury Beauty
Products." *LXMI*, LXMI.com, Web. lxmi.com/.

MacBride, Elizabeth. "How A Minnesota Startup Scaled To
$40 Million Selling U.S.-Manufactured Clothes." *Forbes*,
Forbes Magazine, 5 July 2017, Web. www.forbes.com/sites/
elizabethmacbride/2017/06/30/love-your-melons-founder-
on-how-to-scale-nationally-using-facebook/3/#47332e456740

Mazzoni, Mary. "12 B Corps Leading Their Industries."
Triple Pundit: People, Planet, Profit, TriplePundit.
com, 25 May 2017, Web. www.triplepundit.
com/2016/12/b-corps-leading-their-industries/.

Method. "Benefit Blueprint." *Method Benefit Blueprint*, Method.
com, Web. methodhome.com/benefit-blueprint/.hps://www.
eileenfisher.com/vision-2020/

Mulupi, Dinfin. "Meet the Boss: Jeremy Johnson,
CEO, Andela." *How We Made It In Africa*, DHL, 4
Aug. 2015, Web. www.howwemadeitinafrica.com/
meet-the-boss-jeremy-johnson-ceo-andela/50879/.

Palasz, Emma. "Social Enterprise Brands You Should
Be Watching in 2017." *Prosper Strategies*, Prosper
Strategies, 9 June 2017, Web. prosper-strategies.
com/2017-social-enterprise-brands/.

Primeau, Jamie. "11 Robin Williams' 'Dead Poets Society' Quotes
That Will Inspire You to 'Carpe Diem.'" *Bustle*, Bustle.com,
Web. www.bustle.com/articles/35405-11-robin-williams-dead-
poets-society-quotes-that-will-inspire-you-to-carpe-diem.

Sarumi, Ahrif. "Outdoor Company Cotopaxi Puts Its Money

Where Its Heart Is." *The Huffington Post*, TheHuffingtonPost.
com, 28 Aug. 2014, Web. www.huffingtonpost.com/ahrif-sa-
rumi/cotopaxi-put-its-money-where-its-heart-is_b_5710167.
html.

CHAPTER TEN

Sorkin, Andrew Ross. "BlackRock's Message: Contribute
to Society, or Risk Losing Our Support." *The New York
Times*, The New York Times, 15 Jan. 2018, Web. www.
nytimes.com/2018/01/15/business/dealbook/blackrock-lau-
rence-fink-letter.html.

9 781641 370363